BECOMING
A YOUNG WOMAN OF GOD
JEN RAWSON

AN 8-WEEK CURRICULUM FOR MIDDLE SCHOOL GIRLS

FOR AGES 11-14

ZONDERVAN®

ZONDERVAN.com/
AUTHORTRACKER
follow your favorite authors

youth
specialties

youth specialties

Becoming a Young Woman of God
Copyright 2008 by Jen Rawson

Youth Specialties resources, 300 S. Pierce St., El Cajon, CA 92020 are published by Zondervan, 5300 Patterson Ave. SE, Grand Rapids, MI 49530.

ISBN 978-0-310-27547-3

Cover design by Toolbox Studios
Interior design by Mark Novelli, IMAGO MEDIA

Printed in the United States of America

12 13 • 20 19 18 17 16 15 14 13 12 11 10 9 8

My beauty from the ashes.

Dedicated to the most important girls in my life. Ciera, Charis, Hannah, Alexis, Caroline, and Lillian.

A special thanks to my mom, Rita Harris, for being my example of becoming and living as a godly woman.

CONTENTS

INTRODUCTION: WHY YOU NEED THIS BOOK

It's amazingly easy to convince a middle school girl that she's worthless, that her parents don't understand her, and that everything about her is inadequate. She may be transformed from a girl who a few years prior loved many things and was confident and mostly pleasant to be around into an emotional, dramatic young woman who's obsessed with her appearance and no longer believes in herself. How does this happen? The answer is quite simple. Our culture—television, magazines, movies, music, billboards, the Internet—combined with the pressures of school life and girls' changing bodies, minds, and emotions is a mixture sure to confuse and upset even the most foundationally stable girls. They stop being themselves and start appearing and acting like all the other females around them. They take on the rigorous occupation of evolving into the "ideal woman" by being female impersonators. Then when they see they're failing at the task of becoming ideal women (because they all will), their lives become a mess. What's more, parents are often on their own in this struggle. And when parental advice goes up against the views of friends and the media, guess whose suggestions and concerns are left by the wayside?

Becoming a Young Woman of God is designed to help girls stop pretending and start becoming the young women God created them to be. When they embrace and stay true to that identity, your girls will not only survive this tumultuous transition into womanhood, but they'll also be happy, healthy, and whole. *Becoming a Young Woman of God* creates an opportunity to come alongside parents to mentor girls in the face of our culture and the lies it tells them. It helps you train girls to use the minds God gave them to question and critique what they're seeing, hearing, and reading. It upholds truth—because girls must find value in who they are, as they are; exude authenticity; and have the courage and know-how to analyze life instead of let life happen to them.

WHAT IT IS

Becoming a Young Woman of God is an eight-week curriculum geared toward small groups of middle school girls discipled by adult women. It addresses important foundational aspects of who girls can be at their core, provides principles to live by, and offers ideas to carry out those principles. It begins the task of transforming their thinking from a mentality that values what our culture says to the mind of Christ. From trying to be like all women, they move toward trying to become like Christ.

The goal is for your girls to discover and appreciate how great it is that they're *not* like every other girl out there and to stay on track in the journey toward becoming the women God wants them to be, toward finding their value in Jesus. If your girls can internalize the truth that they're valuable because God created and cares about them, as well as use their minds to process and question what they see and hear, they'll be on track for healthy choices and fulfilling lives. They'll see themselves as truly beautiful because they are becoming "of Christ."

THE METHOD BEHIND THE MADNESS

Ingredients

At the beginning of each session you'll find a list of items you'll need to lead it.

Appetizer

Each session begins with a crazy game or activity that ties into the topic for the week. Sometimes the point is made right away; other times the point of the game/activity is brought up later in the session. When it comes to games, most middle school girls are up for about anything. But occasionally a girl doesn't want to participate. In these cases I always encourage the girl but never force her. If the same girl doesn't want to participate every week, have one of your more mature students personally invite her to get involved. (An invitation from an adult isn't the same as one from a peer.)

Specialty

Each session incorporates activities such as fun quizzes and group projects, age-appropriate crafts, situation scenarios, movie clips, music, and stories. To keep interest high, each session includes the option of using at least one video clip.

Time-limit disclaimer: You may not have the necessary minutes or hours to get through all of the activities in each session from week to week. That's okay! If there's more than one movie clip, and you don't have time for both, just choose the one you like better. The same is true with the other activities. Pick and choose whatever best gets through to your group. If a craft doesn't go well one week, try something else the next. On a low budget? Check out books and movies from the library. Do what works for you.

TAKE OUT

At the end of every session there's a suggested way for the girls to take home what they've learned that day. This is an object of some kind that they can place in their rooms, in their pockets, or in their lockers at school; it will remind them of the truth you all discussed. (What your girls are learning goes against what our culture is teaching them; transforming minds isn't easy. So they need all the reminders they can get!)

Helping parents

I believe our role as leaders is to assist parents. They know their children better than anyone else, and we get the opportunity to assist the experts in molding these girls. So in a few lessons we ask parents to get involved, mostly with helping their daughters with the brainteasers given in the Soul Work, sometimes with the questions in the Soul Work and in one case by sending parents a letter. You'll need to mail the letters for Week Seven ahead of time, as they must be mailed to give parents enough time to respond during the week.

Reality Check (student outlines)

To help your girls stay focused, pass out these reproducible student outlines before each session. They can help your girls remain actively involved in the session as they follow along, fill in the blanks, and answer multiple choice questions, as well as group questions. Plus, when they put pens to paper, they're taking one more step toward cementing truth in their hearts and minds. The student outlines will also be very helpful for the girls during the week while they're doing their Soul Work.

(Note: As you're leading the session and come to a "Reality Check" heading, just prompt your girls by saying "Reality Check" and ask the question or questions or read the statement or verse— your girls have the same wording on their handouts.)

Soul Work

This is a fancy word for *homework*—but because it's homework for the soul, it's much more meaningful than studying for a math quiz. **Soul Work** is done during the week, between meetings. It includes assignments such as critiquing a TV show, interviews, journaling, and many other activities that help your girls think for themselves.

Each **Soul Work** handout starts out with some fun brainteasers that seem to have nothing to do with anything. But be assured they do have a purpose. First, they help the girls look forward to something; second, they encourage them to talk to their parents and siblings about the answers. (Pretty tricky, eh?)

Plus, every week each girl is asked to be in contact with an "other" to reinforce her relationships with parents, grandparents, and mentors. The "other" typically is Mom—a middle school girl's hardest relationship is with her mom. Yet it is by far one of the most important, so we want to help as much as we can to foster that relationship. If we're lucky enough to catch moms and daughters when they aren't struggling with communication, then it will make the relational foundation all the more firm— and will further aid your girls to deal with what's to come.

You'll have some girls who are faithful in doing their **Soul Work** every week; others may never do a single assignment. If girls come with their **Soul Work** incomplete, rather than laying on the guilt, help them through the discussion. And keep encouraging them to do the work since it will allow them to see how what they've learned meets real life, covers material you didn't have time to deal with at the meeting, and helps them get personal and application-oriented with regard to the study sessions. You can review the answers and thoughts the girls came up with—just keep in mind how much time you want to spend reviewing a previous week's **Soul Work** versus leading the current session.

WHY YOU NEED THE NEXT BOOK, TOO!

Don't forget to continue discipling your middle school girls with the sequel to this book, *Living as a Young Woman of God*. Where *Becoming* lays the foundation, *Living* constructs the house, so to speak. It gets really practical with your girls, helping you guide them toward the kind of life God wants them to have. Check it out after you finish the last chapter of *Becoming*.

ONE LAST THOUGHT

You're about to embark on a trip that few women take part in. Middle school students are often forgotten. They're not children but far from adults. They're moody, mouthy...and yet moldable. Their minds are switching from concrete to abstract. They're just starting to question what's real and what isn't. Do they really believe in this God their parents believe in? They're trying to decide which friends they're going to hang around. Most important, they're trying to discover who they are and who they're going to become.

That's when you step in.

CHAPTER ONE

LESS THAN BECOMING: A LOOK AT OUR CULTURE

INGREDIENTS

A bag of dried lentil beans, small pieces of paper with the text of Proverbs 3:5 on one side, blindfolds, video clip on how our culture portrays women (prepare ahead of time), magazines, glue, scissors, poster board, out-of-focus/fuzzy photos.

APPETIZER: LENTIL-BEAN LAND MINES

Instructions: Scatter lentil beans on the floor. Have each girl walk across the "mine field" blindfolded with shoes off. This isn't a race, but you can send more than one person at a time to speed things along. The only directions are that the girls need to get from one side to the other without stepping on the lentil-bean land mines.

After they've all crossed, say something like, **You're growing up in a world that's telling you what it thinks being a woman means. You probably take what life gives you and assume you have no choice as to what happens next. You may let life happen to you instead of thinking through what life has to offer, instead of choosing what life you will live. You then stop becoming who God created you to be and start trying to be what others want you to be.**

Continue, **It's like these "land mines." They make it awkward to walk, but you kept on moving anyway. None of you tried to get away from the land mines. In the same way, it's hard on your soul and your true self to go through life in our culture. It's as if you're blindfolded, and the world around you is full of "bombs" that blow up who God wants you to be.**

APPETIZER: VIDEO CLIP

Show the video on our culture you prepared—it can include commercials, MTV, or anything you feel shows how women are portrayed in our culture. (You can also use go to www.campaignforrealbeauty.com and watch the clip titled "onslaught.")

After the clip is over say, **Obviously, we're bombarded with messages and images of what we should be as women. Let's look deeper.**

Ask, **What makes you a woman? When does a girl become a woman?** *(Possible answers: When she starts her period, when she first has sex, when she starts to wear makeup, when she can date, when she first goes to college, when she first lives on her own, when she first wears a bra, when she gets married, etc.)*

Then say something like, **We're going to keep working on this answer over the next couple of weeks. This week let's see what the world tells us a woman is.**

SPECIALTY: MAGAZINE COLLAGE

Instructions: Pass out glue, scissors, and poster board and have your girls create collages using pictures and words from magazines *(Seventeen, J-14, Cosmo Girl; People, Us, and Glamour are all good choices).* to answer the questions "What makes you a woman?" and "When does a girl become a woman?" (This is best done as a group or in small groups. However, if you're short on time, you can prepare a collage in advance to show them. But if you're able, give them plenty of time—about 15 minutes.)

Some things I found were:

▷ Photos of girls in inappropriate clothes

▷ Many article titles about how to get "that guy"

▷ How to look sexier

▷ Ways to make your man happy

▷ Millions of makeup ads

▷ How to get the body you want

▷ Girls in seductive poses

▷ Provocative cartoons

▷ Materialism galore

▷ Which celebrities pose nude

▷ Where to find the hottest parties

▷ Makeover tips

Tip: Be sure to keep the finished collages. Use them as decorations in your youth room to refer back to often as reminders of what you and the girls are discussing. Other lessons will also refer back to the collages.

QUESTIONS AND COMMENTARY

After the collages are finished, say, **Think of yourself as an alien studying America for the first time. Your crew is getting ready to morph into beings that look just like young American women. It's your job to do the research for your crew so you all don't get found out. You haven't had any contact with American females; you've only been able to look at these magazines. With that in mind, see what conclusions you're able to draw from question 1.**

Reality Check

1. **If you were an alien studying American culture...**

   A. **What kinds of women are respected?**

   B. **What's the normal body shape?**

   C. **What's a female's role?**

   D. **What are women's interests?**

After some time, say, **This is how magazines portray the "ideal" woman. What about other types of media—TV, billboards, music, music videos, etc.? What are they presenting for you? If we could make a collage of these media, what would it look like?**

After some discussion give each student a few minutes alone to answer questions two, three, and four on their Reality Check sheets.

2. **What does this teach you about your role and value as a woman in America?**

3. **How do you feel about all of this?**

4. **Do you ever get tired of trying to live up to what the world says you should be?**

Leader Note: *Oddly, when asked something like question four, most girls will say they don't feel the pressure. Why? Some haven't hit puberty yet. They're just discovering boys. The culture's pressure that girls fit into a "perfect woman" mold isn't too huge yet. Others, however, may not see anything wrong with this perfect-woman stereotype. Maybe they've bought into what culture's preaching. If they're giving the typical answer (that they don't feel pressure to live up to what the culture says they should be), challenge them. Ask each girl to tell you one thing she doesn't like about her body. Is there a celebrity she'd just die to look like? Has she ever felt ugly because a guy didn't like her? In any case, don't let the girls get away with thinking they really don't care that our culture's telling them who they're supposed to be, how to behave, and what to look like. You might even take a survey of what everyone in the room is wearing to prove your point.*

Reality Check

5. Do you think you'll ever get there?

Leader Note: *This stuff doesn't just go away because you grow up. Cosmo Girl turns into Cosmo, and J-14 turns into Seventeen, which then turns into Elle. The desire to look good never really stops. Tell a story about how you struggle even now. Look at those alien questions again and see if any of them are true. Just discuss these briefly (they're discussed more heavily next week).*

Then say, **This all leads to one more question: What happens when you don't fit this role or appearance? Because most of us won't all the time.**

After you receive some answers, say, **Now check out this verse:**

Reality Check

6. Proverbs 14:12 says, "There is a way that appears to be <u>right</u>, but in the end it leads to <u>death</u>."

Ask, **How does the way our culture views women and what it expects from women lead to death?** *(Possible answers: It could be a literal death for some, such as runaway teenagers living in prostitution, girls who end up with AIDS, doing drugs, or anorexia.)*

Then ask, **What other kinds of death could the verse mean?** After some answers and discussion say something like, **The Bible often talks about death and life in ways meaning true happiness and joy that only come from a relationship with Christ and living within his safety. In that context what does this verse mean?**

After some answers say, **Look at your collage. Where's the information on how to get along with Mom and Dad, deepen your spiritual life, be a better friend (a real one), study more effectively, better your character, be happy with the way your body already is, be kind to the people who drive you nuts, deal with all of the feelings and emotions you experience as a middle schooler, what to do when your parents get a divorce?**

Then say, **Instead culture focuses on how you can look skinnier, prettier, and sexier. Wear the right stuff. Act ditzy and flirt more. Culture doesn't care about *you*. Many forces in our culture will kill your self, joy, and happiness and give you no help with real life. When we focus on what our culture tells us, we stop being happy with how we look and start trying to look like everyone else. We see models in magazines and try to copy their hairstyles. We see someone looking good in a pair of jeans, and we assume if we get those same jeans, we, too, will look good and get attention.**

Reality Check

7. **Female impersonators:**

   A. **What's an impersonation?**

   B. **What does a female impersonator do?**

   C. **Do you ever feel like you're being a female impersonator?**

   D. **In what ways do you see girls trying to be like everyone else?**

After some time, say, **In the movie *13 Going on 30*, there's a scene where Jenna's at her 13th birthday party, trying to be cool for the other girls and the cool guys. Her best friend is a dorky overweight boy—but he calls her a robot. What do you think he means?**

After getting some answers, say, **Do you know why you can stop trying so hard to be female impersonators? Because you're already females. Don't impersonate someone else—be yourself.**

Reality Check

8. Isaiah 55:8 says, "For my <u>thoughts</u> are not your thoughts, neither are your ways my <u>ways</u>."

Specialty: Fuzzy Photos

Instructions: Snap some out-of-focus photos yourself or find some on the Internet and print them or place them in a PowerPoint program. (The photos can be of anything. The point is that we only see a small part of a bigger idea. For instance, if your item is a pencil, then you'd want the photo to be of the sharpened lead point—and out of focus.) Have students guess what the blurry pictures are.

Then say, **God does things differently than we do. We can clearly see in our collages how the world values women and girls. But God sees things differently. And even though it makes sense to you to dress as our culture requires and act the way our culture tells you to—and find value in those things—God sees life differently...and sees clearly in all the places where we can't! Our vision is blurry—just like these pictures. God's thoughts aren't the same as ours.**

Then ask, **Have you ever thought you had something in life all figured out and then later said, "Well, if I'd known that, then I would've..."?**

After any discussion say, **God knows it all already and has something to say about what our culture tells us is okay. We can't always understand or see clearly why God says do this or that or don't, but that's what trust is all about.**

Reality Check

9. Proverbs 3:5-6: "<u>Trust</u> in the LORD with all your heart and lean not on your own understanding; in all your ways submit to him, and he will make your <u>paths</u> straight."

SPECIALTY: LAND MINE REPRISE

Let your girls walk through the lentil-bean land mines again—only this time without blindfolds. The only rule this time is that the girls have to stay in the land-mine area...just like we have to live in this world.

Ask, **How was this time different?**

After your girls answer, say, **What we're going to do during the next few weeks together is like taking off the blindfolds to cross these land mines. We're going to help open your eyes so you can see and be able to live in this culture without it wearing you down. So even when no one else understands why you aren't like them, why you dress differently, act differently, or talk differently, you can know you're going to be happier, healthier, and whole because of being different. I hope to help you see with God's eyes so you can see clearly where everyone else sees a fuzzy picture. But others will be walking on "bombs" and getting hurt, while you'll be able to walk around the bombs and be protected from some of the damage our culture can cause.**

TAKE OUT

Give each girl one of the tiny pieces of paper with the text from Proverbs 3:5—this will help remind her to keep her eyes open and start looking at the world differently.

CLOSING ACTIVITY: EXPLAIN SOUL WORK

Say, **We'll be having Soul Work every week to help you process what we're talking about. We'll be journaling, filling out quizzes, doing multiple-choice questions, and even interviewing friends and other people. This is fun, not work. That's why we'll call it Soul Work instead of homework. You'll have the opportunity to share your ideas and thoughts when we meet as a group. All I ask is that you be completely honest and spend time truly thinking about your answers. The more effort you put into Soul Work, the more you'll grow and become who God designed you to be.**

Pass out **Soul Work** sheets, then close in prayer.

LESS THAN BECOMING: A LOOK AT OUR CULTURE

1. If you were an alien studying American culture...

    A. What kinds of women are respected?

    B. What's the normal body shape?

    C. What's a female's role?

    D. What are women's interests?

2. What does this teach you about your role and value as a woman in America?

3. How do you feel about all of this?

4. Do you ever get tired of trying to live up to what the world says you should be?

5. Do you think you'll ever get there?

6. Proverbs 14:12 says, "There is a way that appears to be _____, but in the end it leads to_____."

7. Female impersonators:

    A. What's an impersonation?

B. What does a female impersonator do?

C. Do you ever feel like you're being a female impersonator?

D. In what ways do you see girls trying to be like everyone else?

8. Isaiah 55:8 says, "For my_____ are not your thoughts, neither are your ways my_____."

9. Proverbs 3:5-6: "_____ in the LORD with all your heart and lean not on your own understanding; in all your ways submit to him, and he will make your_____ straight."

LESS THAN BECOMING: A LOOK AT OUR CULTURE

Every week I want to get your brain moving and your pens grooving. This first week I'll let you be the one who knows the answer!

Brainteaser

Find a friend or parent and try this out. Have him pick a number, keeping it a secret. Then have him double it, then multiply it by five, and then tell you that number. All you have to do is knock off the final digit and you'll have his original number. Be sure to practice on your own first so you can see that it works.

Soul Work questions

Okay, now that you have those brain juices flowing, let's get started. You're going to evaluate television. Pick one or two shows you regularly watch or enjoy watching when you have a chance. (Wait until your parents find out that your "assignment" for church is to watch TV!) You'll want to grab a pen. As you watch this show, try to be like the aliens we pretended to be when we made our collages in class. You're going to evaluate how media is trying to portray women in our culture. See what TV is telling you personally about what you should be. TV teaches good things and bad things, so look for both.

Here are some questions to answer while you watch your show.

1. How are the women dressed?

2. What role(s) do(es) the character(s) play? If there's more than one female character who plays a significant role in the show, circle all that apply.

Funny	Sexy
Strong	Dorky
Wife	Seductive
Intelligent	Desperate
Stupid	Independent
Loving	Rude

3. How do men respond to her/them?

4. How do women respond to her/them?

5. What does this teach you about your value as a woman in America?

6. Finish this sentence according to your own thoughts (not according to the show you watched). To be the "perfect woman" I need to...

7. Ask an adult woman (preferably your mom) when she thinks a girl becomes a woman. Write down her answer.

8. How do the women on TV, in movies, and in magazines get to be so perfect?

CHAPTER TWO

START BECOMING: EXPOSING LIES AND EMBRACING TRUTH

INGREDIENTS

Index cards, examples of digitally retouched photos, "Model Evolution" video clip (if possible to download or play from the Web), pages from *Victoria's Secret* catalog, Switchfoot's CD *The Beautiful Letdown* and printed-out lyrics to "This Is Your Life" from the CD, art supplies, inexpensive paintbrushes (one per girl), tape measure

REVIEW SOUL WORK

Every week you're going to talk through the answers on their **Soul Work.** You don't need to have every person answer every question. This time is to help the girls be accountable for doing their work as well as to be sure they understand what you're talking about. It's also fun to see moments where lights came on about what you've been discussing. Give them a chance to share their answers to the questions you think are hot topics for your group. The ability to share their answers will help the girls see that they have valuable insights and teach each other that it's okay to question life. Be sure to commend those who did the **Soul Work**. A candy reward will work wonders. Also, don't shame those who didn't do it; simply encourage them to do it next week.

This week spend a fair amount of time discussing their evaluations of TV shows. How do they feel about what they watched? Do they think there's anything wrong with what they saw? This will help you get a grasp on where your girls are. Never be afraid to question them or challenge their thinking. Also ask them how the brainteaser went.

APPETIZER

Say something like, **Today we're going to play a game to test your lying abilities. On your index card I want you to write two truths and one lie. They can be in any order but try to make them things people here wouldn't know about you. When you finish, we'll take turns sharing what we wrote and guessing which statements are the lies.**

After the activity say, **Sometimes it's hard to tell the truth from a lie. So today we're going to expose some lies you may not know about.**

Ask, **What does "model student" mean to you? How about "model citizen"? "Model child"?**

After you receive some answers, say, **These are statuses anyone can attain with enough hard work and discipline. So then what's a "supermodel"?**

After you receive some answers, give your own: **Someone who shows us the perfect way to look.**

QUESTIONS AND COMMENTARY

Reality Check

1. **John 8:32 says, "Then you will know the <u>truth</u> and the truth will set you <u>free</u>."**

   Ask, **What does this verse mean to you?**

   After you receive some answers, say, **Knowing the truth helps you deal with life in many ways. How does this verse apply to siding with our culture's standards versus God's standards?**

   After you receive some answers, say, **So let's look at some truth.**

   Ask, **Do you remember from last week our alien questions for our collage:**

   > *What kinds of women are respected?*

   > *What's the normal body shape?*

   > *What's a female's role?*

   > *What are women's interests?*

   Say, **We can answer a few of these for sure right now.**

   Have your girls guess out loud the statistics through #5 on their Reality Check outlines as you read (i.e., say "blank" instead of your underlined stats).

Reality Check

2. If *supermodel* means the perfect-looking woman, let's see what, in fact, she looks like.

   A. The average model stands <u>5'10"</u> tall. She weighs <u>105</u> pounds. She wears a size <u>zero to four</u>.

Ask, **Do any of you match any of these measurements?** (In most middle school groups you'll have girls the same weight or clothes size but not the same height. Even if you have an adult who's the right height, she probably doesn't fit the other two measurements.)

Next get out a measuring tape and mark on the wall how tall 5'10" really is.

Now say, **All you have to do is keep growing but not let your bones get any heavier or not get any more muscles because they weigh more than fat. In fact, you'd better consider chopping off an arm or something because to add that much height yet stay the same weight is going to require losing a limb or two.**

Ask, **Any guesses as to the height, weight, and clothes size of the average American woman?** After some guesses reveal the stats of the average grown woman.

Reality Check

B. The average woman stands <u>5'4" to 5'5"</u> tall. She weighs <u>145</u> pounds and wears a size <u>12 to 14</u>.

Say, **You can work hard and starve yourself into 105 pounds as a grown adult; however, I've never seen anyone stretch their bones five to six inches.**

Reality Check

3. Marilyn Monroe (the "perfect woman" in the 1950s who Anna Nicole Smith idolized) wore a size <u>12</u>.

4. If <u>Barbie</u> were real, she'd have to walk on all fours to support her proportions.

5. Of about <u>three</u> <u>billion</u> women only about <u>eight</u> naturally look like supermodels.

After you've revealed all the stats, say, **In case you haven't gotten the idea yet, a supermodel isn't the best and most accurate model of how we should look. Yet the world keeps telling us they are, and the way we look and the importance of female bodies have reached all-time high levels. It's gotten so out of hand, even the celebrities and models aren't good enough anymore. Check these out:**

Michelle Pfeiffer was on the cover of *Esquire* magazine once with an article titled "What Michelle Pfeiffer Needs Is Absolutely Nothing." She looked perfect. The ironic part was what she actually did need. Here's a list of where the $1,525 spent on photo touch-ups went: *Clean up complexion, soften eye lines, soften smile line, add color to lips, trim chin, remove neck lines, soften line under earlobe, add highlights to earrings, add blush to cheek, clean up neck line, remove stray hair, remove hair strand on dress, adjust color and add hair on top of head, add dress to side to create better line, add dress on shoulder, clean up and smooth dress folds under arm and create one seam on image of right side, add forehead to create better line, remove red dress at corner of neck, add dress on shoulder to sharpen and create a better line, soften neck muscle a bit, and soften neck line on image on left side.*

Then say, **All of this was after she'd already been made up by hair and makeup specialists.**

SPECIALTY: DIGITAL TOUCH-UPS

Now show the girls other examples of digital touch-ups. (I created some "before and after" shots just with my Photoshop software. You can also show some professional examples from this incredible Web site: http://homepage.mac.com/gapodaca/digital/digital.html. I also found a couple of articles online to show my girls.)

Option: Show the "Model Evolution" clip from Dove's www.campaignforrealbeauty.com. After you've shown the clip once, let your girls see the before shot at 0:05 and the after shot at 0:36.

Now say, **The July 2003 issue of *Redbook* had a picture of Julia Roberts with an article titled "The Real Julia." The picture was of Julia; however, her head and body were cropped together from two different pictures. Jennifer Aniston had the same thing done to her. Oprah has appeared on magazines with her head on someone else's body! Tyra Banks was quoted as saying, "I disappoint** people who meet me in person because I do not look like me." Cindy Crawford was quoted as saying, "I don't look like Cindy Crawford when I wake up in the morning." No wonder I don't feel as if I look good next to these supermodels. They don't even look good next to themselves.

Reality Check

6. How do you feel about digital touch-ups?

After the girls have had some time to answer, ask, **What do you think about all of this? Do you ever get tired of trying to live up to what the world says you should be like? Do you think you'll ever get there?**

Say, **These are similar to some questions we asked last week: How honest were you then? How honest are you being now? How have your opinions changed?**

After some discussion read this scenario: **If someone were to give you $100 to publish a picture your dad took of you without any digital touch-ups, would you agree? This picture would be seen by everyone you know: your old boyfriends, your friends who haven't seen you in a while, the girl who totally makes fun of you. What if the picture was taken on a day you weren't feeling so great about yourself? Maybe you woke up with a big zit on your nose, or the one thing you like least about yourself stuck out huge in this picture. Would you still do it? It was even going in the yearbook!**

After you get some answers, pull out the pages you chose ahead of time from your *Victoria's Secret* catalog (not the whole catalog). Say, **Taking into consideration all the digital touch-ups already done to these women, check out what a simple bra can do.** (*Leader Hint:* Look through your catalog ahead of time and find the same model in a picture wearing a push-up bra and another picture of her in a normal shirt showing her with a regular-sized chest. Make the point that with all of today's bras that push up and push together, add gel and padding, and do whatever else the manufacturers come up with, you don't need only digital touch-ups to compete with the lies of the world. Most of the breasts we see are lies as well.)

Say, **Last week we looked at what media says women are for. We saw how we're expected to look, and many of you saw on TV how we're supposed to act. We're being fed lies every day, and as you saw with the digital retouching, we can no longer tell what's real and not real.**

Continue, **You're entering a season in your life where all this stuff—looks, boys, feelings, friends, etc.—is a huge part of who you want to be. Maybe you're starting to hate your body and get frustrated with how you respond to people and situations. If you do something embarrassing, it feels like the end of the world. If your friends ditch you, it can make you feel worthless. If a boy rejects you, he suddenly has the power to make you feel ugly. You're entering or have already entered an important time for becoming who God intends you to be.**

Now say, **Female impersonators are all around you. They're the women and girls who are trying to be supermodels. They're trying to change their bodies to look like supermodels' bodies. They act flirtatious and sexy like women they see on TV. They dress in ways that'll seduce males because this is what our culture says we're supposed to do. They see the magazine covers, which aren't real, and they see shows on TV, which aren't real, and they try to become those people. We all seem like the same person. Almost like robots. We may be different models of robot, but we all follow the same basic idea, do the same basic tasks, and sound basically the same way.**

Then say, **As we revealed at the last meeting, you're already a female, so you can stop trying so hard. All that stuff you see on TV and in magazines and other media isn't real. Now you know the truth. But how can this truth set you free?**

Reality Check

7. 1 Samuel 16:7 says, "The LORD does not look at the things <u>human beings</u> look at. People look at the outward appearance, but the LORD looks at the <u>heart</u>."

Ask, **Is the truth in this verse hard for you to remember? Why or why not? So how do we make this verse a part of who we are?**

Reality Check

A. **Be aware. Romans 12:2 says, "Do not conform any longer to the pattern of this world, but be transformed by the <u>renewing</u> of your <u>mind</u>."**

Say, **You could say it like this: Retrain your mind. Don't allow yourself to think that way. When you catch yourself thinking about outer appearance, stop and think of five good qualities about yourself or the person you're thinking of.**

Reality Check

B. **Look for <u>heroes</u>.**

Ask, **Who do you respect and why? What are things you admire about your mom or another female you highly respect? Their looks or their deeds and values?**

Reality Check

C. **Choose to look at your <u>heart</u>.**

Say, **It all comes down to this: Do you want to live your life looking in mirrors, hating who you see because you'll never measure up? Will this bring you true and complete happiness?**

Then say, **For the next several weeks I'm going to challenge the world around you. I'm going to help you think about all these lies you're being told. God's going to show you that you belong to heaven, and that's all that matters. God knows how he created you. God wants to see you at your best. God wants you to be free from the stronghold of this world.**

Play the song "This Is Your Life" by Switchfoot (find the lyrics online and print them for your group to follow while the track is playing).

Say, **This is your life. You determine who you are. Don't settle for less than what you want or for becoming less than the beautiful woman God plans for you to be. These next several weeks I'm going to help you do this. I'm going to help you evaluate as many areas of your lives as you can. This can be a time of truly growing up for you.**

TAKE OUT

Pass out some fun art supplies and a sheet of blank paper to each girl. Have the girls write "John 8:32" on their papers as well as the words "This is my life." Let them decorate their papers so they can put them up in their rooms, in their lockers, or on their mirrors. Glue a paintbrush to the front of each page as a reminder of the touch-ups all around us. Give each student a few minutes to write out a prayer on the back of her page. Encourage the girls to ask God for the ability to see truth. Invite one girl to read her prayer in closing.

START BECOMING: EXPOSING LIES AND EMBRACING TRUTH

1. John 8:32 says, "Then you will know the_____ and the truth will set you_____."

2. If *supermodel* means the perfect-looking woman, let's see what, in fact, she looks like.

   A. The average model stands_____ tall. She weighs_____ pounds. She wears a size_____.

   B. The average woman stands _____ tall. She weighs_____ pounds and wears a size_____.

3. Marilyn Monroe wore a size_____.

4. If_____ were real, she'd have to walk on all fours to support her proportions.

5. Of about_____ women only about_____ naturally look like supermodels.

6. How do you feel about digital touch-ups?

7. 1 Samuel 16:7 says, "The LORD does not look at the things_____ look at. People look at the outward appearance, but the LORD looks at the_____."

   A. Be aware. Romans 12:2 says, "Do not conform any longer to the pattern of this world, but be transformed by the_____ of your_____.

   B. Look for_____.

   C. Choose to look at your_____.

START BECOMING: EXPOSING LIES AND EMBRACING TRUTH

Brainteaser

What do these mean?

1. Sun., Mon., Tues., Thurs., Fri., Sat._____

2. RRRRRRR   RRRRRRR   RRRRRRR   RRRRRRR   RRRRRRR   RRRRRRR
   RRRRRRR_____

3. 2th DK_____

4. Every Right Thing_____

5. ALL 0_____

Soul Work questions

1. How do you feel about digital retouching? Did you know about this lie in our culture?

2. Why do we all try to look and act the same?

3. Do you have any heroes? Who are they?

4. Who are some women you know personally who you respect and look up to?

5. What do you admire about these women?

6. Do you admire the same things about your heroes?

7. Call an adult woman in your life who you really respect and think of as sort of a hero or someone you'd like to be like someday. Be sure to write down her responses so we can all hear her wisdom. Ask her these two questions and write down her answers.

   A. What do you think the key is to keep you from getting wrapped up in what others think about you?

B. What are the three things you value most in life?

8. This is your life—are you who you want to be? (You can just think about this one; you don't need to answer.)

CHAPTER THREE

BECOMING WISE: CHOICES

REVIEW SOUL WORK

Remember our goal is to encourage those who did their work and extend grace to those who didn't. Here are the answers to the brainteasers. Did you get them?

1. A week with one day off

2. Forty-niners

3. Tooth decay

4. Right between everything

5. Nothing after all

APPETIZER

I use Doug Fields' *Would You Rather...?* on a regular basis. If you don't have a copy, it's a quick question book that gives students on-the-spot choices ("Would you rather...?") between, for example, sitting on a thumbtack or eating a live cricket. For this activity either use questions from *Would You Rather...?* or make up your own. Have your girls sit in a circle and take turns answering the questions; have them move to the left or right depending on the answer. If someone's in a chair a girl needs to move to, lap-sitting is allowed.

When the activity has concluded, say, **The last couple of weeks we've asked the question "What makes you become a woman?" Today we're going to talk about one of the major things that separates girls from women. Any guesses? Here's a hint: The answer relates to what you did in the game we just finished. Check out** this verse in 1 Corinthians 13:11: "When I was a child, I talked like a child, I thought like a child, I reasoned like a child. When I became a [wo]man, I put the ways of a childhood behind me." (Put the emphasis on [wo].) **Give up?**

If no one has answered correctly, say, **What childish ways do you think Paul is referring to in the verse I just read? It sounds to me like he's talking about thoughts and reasoning...that is, choices. Making good choices truly separates the girls from the women.**

QUESTIONS AND COMMENTARY

Reality Check

1. **When you start making good <u>choices</u> and put your childish ways behind you, you've entered into womanhood.**

   Say, **If you could do this on a regular basis, your life would be revolutionized. So let's learn how.**

Specialty

Prepare to show clips from the DVD of *13 Going on 30*.

Explain the plot, saying something like, **The movie starts with Jenna at her birthday party. She's bribed the cool girls, called "the six chicks," to come in return for her writing their papers for them. At the party she totally puts down her best friend Matt, who's chubby and somewhat of a dork. Then the cool girls trick her into thinking she's going to be in the closet with the boy she likes. Jenna goes into the closet, and the six chicks leave her alone in there. When Matt finds her, Jenna is humiliated and goes back into the closet wishing she was 30. She gets her wish. As she starts to realize this isn't a dream, she tracks down Matt.** Show chapter nine (three minutes). Say, **She thinks she has it all.**

Then say, **Jenna later starts to see who she has become. She's sad about the choices she's made over her 30 years, and even though she seems to have it all, she doesn't like who she has become.** Show chapter 17 (first rewind to Jenna sitting in her house; play DVD until she walks away from Matt, three minutes). Explain, **She goes home to visit her past.** Fast-forward to pancakes with Mom (one minute).

Now say, **Jenna's mom helps her realize she can use her mistakes to learn and start making good choices. She starts to discover who she wants to be and who she was created to be deep down. Meanwhile the high-glamour magazine she works for is dying, and they're looking for ways to keep it alive. She decides to try to show who she is through her work.** Show chapter 24—stop at cheering (two minutes).

Say, **That's what we're working toward—discovering who we really are and being happy about how God made us. Happiness may seem to come from having it all, but if you're not who God created you to be, you won't find happiness. Many people look back on their lives and wish they could do this or that differently. You're not 30 and trying to find out what happened to you; you can't wish and move around in time. You can, however, make good choices now.**

CHOICES

Reality Check

2. **Often the hardest part of making a choice is not the actual <u>doing</u> but <u>deciding</u> what you'll do.**

   Say, **This is like "Would you rather?"—except in real life, choices are more difficult. So you weigh the pros and cons, consider the consequences, and form a plan. Some choices are easy and some are extremely hard. No matter what the choice is, you must decide for yourself. For example, what do I wear to the dance I know the guy I like will be at? You may take days to decide but only a couple of minutes to put the clothes on.**

Reality Check

3. **With a partner answer these questions.**

   A. What are some easy choices you have every day?

   1.

   2.

   3.

   4.

B. What are some hard choices you have every day?

1.

2.

3.

4.

Give the girls a few minutes to write down their choices.

Say, **You can never really escape making choices. Some people try to cop out by not choosing.**

Reality Check

4. If you choose <u>not</u> to choose, you're still making a <u>choice</u>.

Specialty

For this activity give each girl a coin to flip. Have the girls answer the questions on their **Reality Check** sheets according to what they flip on their coins. Heads is yes and tails no unless otherwise noted (H = heads, T = tails). A low-cost option would be to use pennies instead of quarters.

Reality Check

5. For the next few questions flip a coin to determine your future. If you get heads, that means YES. If you get tails, that means NO (unless H or T appears in the question).

Good luck—your future depends on the answers!

A. Will I get to be homecoming queen?

B. Am I going to pass science this year?

C. Will I totally humiliate myself at lunch tomorrow?

D. Will I get married?

E. Will I graduate from college?

F. Will I have (H) two kids or (T) 10 kids?

G. Am I going to have a dead-end job when I'm 30?

H. Will I live in (H) a mansion or (T) a shack?

I. Am I going to stab my friend in the back?

J. Do I like pizza?

K. Do I like the guy sitting closest to me in math?

L. Should I start going by the nickname Oprah?

M. Am I going to rob the lunch lady?

N. Am I going to cheat on the next history exam?

After the girls have had some time to answer on their outlines, say, **Some of these things seem crazy to decide by the flip of a coin. However, we often do just that. We might decide things based on what someone else says. You may decide to rob the lunch lady because someone dared you or cheat on the next history test because someone convinced you it would be a good idea—in other words, you basically "flipped a coin." But you're still responsible for the choices you make regardless of how you decide.**

Ask, **What are some ways you let others make choices for you?**

After you receive some answers, say, **Have you ever heard "you reap what you sow"? This is actually from the Bible. What do you think it means?**

After you receive some answers, say, **Our choices will bring good or bad consequences. For instance, let's try some if-then statements. I'll read the "if" statement; you reply with what you think the "then" statement should be. Ready? (Possible answers are in parentheses and italics.)**

▷ *If* I do my chores before Mom gets home...(then *I don't get grounded*).

▷ *If* I don't get my chores done before Mom gets home...(then *I'll be grounded and won't get to go to the dance I know the guy I like will be at*).

▷ *If* I practice my piano at home...(then *I'll get better and my lesson will go well*).

▷ *If* I don't practice my piano at home...(then *I will still stink at it and I'll have to fake my way through my lesson*).

Say, **In other words,**

Reality Check

6. **A great deal of what <u>happens</u> to us we cause directly or in-directly through our <u>choices</u> (though there are exceptions, such as <u>abuse</u> or if your parents <u>divorced</u>).**

   Leader Note: *You need to go above and beyond here to make sure your girls understand there are exceptions, such as the ones listed. Because if there's abuse or recent divorce in a girl's family, she may not hear you say it's not her fault. Therefore also say,* **Some things happen to us that aren't our fault. If your parents divorce, if you move, if someone dies, or—as we wrote in the blank—if you suffer abuse, obviously you had no choice, and it's not your fault. However, many day-to-day things in life do happen because of the choices we make.**

   Continue, **Let's try some more examples. I'll say the "if" part, and you say the "then" part.**

   ▷ **If I don't shower, then…**

   ▷ **If I'm honest with my parents, then…**

   ▷ **If I get my homework done, then…**

   ▷ **If I don't get my homework done, then…**

   ▷ **If I eat a bowl of worms, then…**

   Ask, **Can you think of some other examples where you reap what you sow in your everyday life?**

   After you receive some answers, say, **We sometimes forget we have choices. We let life happen and play it by ear. But you'll never be truly fulfilled in life or become who God intends if you just let life happen to you. Let me give you a verse as a guide for every decision you make.**

Reality Check

7. **Colossians 2:8 says, "Don't let <u>others</u> spoil your faith and joy with their philosophies, wrong and shallow answers based on men's thoughts and ideas, instead of on what Christ has said" (LB).**

Say, **Read this verse again with me out loud.**

Then ask, **Are you letting others influence your choices based on ungodly ideas, or are you basing what you decide on what God says?**

After a moment say, **Because YOU reap what YOU sow—it's time to grab hold of this truth. Remember—the truth will set you free. You must distinguish between others' voices and your own.**

Then say, **Too often we rely on what our friends do to determine what we do. What our friends like we like. What our friends wear we wear. Even if we think a guy is cute, funny, and totally nice, we decide not to go out with him if our friends think he's a total geek. What do** *you* **think, feel, want, love? You aren't your friends. Are you letting others spoil your joy because they think differently than you? You're an individual God created—why become some-one else? You, not your friends, will reap the consequences—good and bad—for your choices. Be bold and be willing to think for yourself.**

Now ask, **Are the choices you make now easier or harder than the choices when you were in first grade?**

After you receive some answers, say, **The older you get, the hard-er the choices you make. So start making good choices now to prepare yourself for when choices become more difficult. But the great thing is that even though some choices are totally hard, you're not alone. You must learn to hear God's voice.**

Reality Check

8. **Isaiah 30:21 says, "Whether you turn to the right or to the left, your ears will hear a voice behind you saying, 'This is the way; <u>walk in it.</u>'"**

   Ask, **What do you think this verse is saying?** After you receive some answers, say, **God's telling you what you should do. God will help you. Be still. Listen. And use your brain.**

   Say, **How do you hear that small voice? You have this thing called a conscience. It's a good indicator of when God's telling you something. You can listen to the things trusted adults tell you. You can think for yourself. Does a particu-lar choice make sense with everything else you know about**

God? Obviously, God doesn't want you to cheat on a test. And God doesn't want you to wear to a dance something that's not modest and robs you of your value.

Now say, **Choices matter. Little lies lead to big lies. Small thefts lead to larger thefts. Little courage leads to greater courage. These are all choices. And good choices in small decisions lead to good choices in big decisions later on.**

Reality Check

9. **By yourself circle the characteristics or choices that answer "Who do I want to be?"**

Nice	Healthy	Musical
Rude	Peacemaker	Wise
Loving	Hard worker	Intelligent
Arrogant	Intolerant	Creative
Prideful	Racist	Addict
Liar	Exclusive	Gossiper
Godly	Taker	Thief
Honest	Thoughtful	Sweet
Selfish	Accepting	Bitter
Giving	Joyful	Angry
Humble	Patient	Vengeful
Bully	Faithful	Jealous
Annoying	Foolish	Ignorant
Athletic	Hateful	Fight for what is right
Popular	Leader	Self-controlled
Listener	Follower	Compassionate
Pure	Admirable	
Good student	Loyal	

After your girls have had some time to finish, say, **None of us will become any of these things without making choices. Often becoming who we want to be involves hard choices. In the movie Jenna has no idea how she's become the awful person she is at 30. She's made choices without thinking about the consequences. She's become who "the six chicks" wanted her to be. Her self at 30 is the result. Thankfully, she's able to review her life and change.** Ask, **What helps her change?**

After you receive some answers, say, **She has to make choices to change. She decides who she wants to be, and she has to choose to be true to who God made her to be. She loses some friends and some respect from others. What does she gain?**

After you receive some answers, say, **Just like Jenna in our movie takes the opportunity to stop and make the changes needed to be who she wants to be, we should always be asking ourselves, "Am I acting like the person I want to be?"**

Reality Check

10. **How do I become that person?**

Ask, **How do you become the person you want to be 20 years from now or even today?**

Have your girls fill in the blanks on their **Reality Check** sheets.

A. **Determine priorities and <u>values</u>.**

B. **Set <u>goals</u>.**

C. **Establish <u>boundaries</u>.**

D. **<u>Reward</u> yourself for victories.**

Then say, **This week we're going to look at the first of these.**

Reality Check

11. **Determine priorities and values.**

Ask, **What is a value?** Webster tells us…

A. **Something you desire more when <u>compared</u> to other things.**

B. **Something you rate/think <u>highly</u> of.**

Ask the following questions out loud to help the girls begin thinking about some of the things they value. (They don't have to answer; they're on this week's **Soul Work** as well.)

▷ **If my house were on fire, what would I grab while I was escaping?**

▷ **What do I want to accomplish with my day, year, schooling, career, family, life?**

▷ **What things are important to me now? In the future?**

▷ **What are things I won't give up?**

▷ **Who do I want to be?**

▷ **What are things I want to change about myself?**

▷ **What do I need in any relationship?**

▷ **What do I believe in?**

▷ **Are there areas in my faith I won't compromise?**

▷ **What am I really proud of about myself?**

Give them a minute to answer 11 C on their **Reality Check** sheets:

C. **What is VERY, VERY important to me?**

Then say, **You can value many things. What's one thing you value?**

After you receive some answers, say, **We started our time today with the game "Would you rather?" I have one more for you to think over: Would you rather be 30 and happy with who you've become or 30 and ashamed of the person you've become? Seems like an easy answer, but most middle school girls are making choices every day that might lead them to be ashamed of who they'll be at 30. What things that are important to you do you need to reevaluate? Do you need to find new priorities and set new values so you can be the person you want to be? This is your life! It's your choice.**

Begin to wrap up the meeting by saying, **This week's Soul Work is going to help you continue to discover some of the things you value. Ask God to reveal some things to you. Then try to listen and be aware of what God may be telling you. When** you know what you value, then you can work to be sure you don't compromise those things by the decisions you make.

Really encourage this week's **Soul Work**. Let your girls know that they'll be using their values for next week's lesson. This may even be a good week to call your students midweek and remind them to do the work, as well as offer to help them if they're stuck.

TAKE OUT

Say, **I want you each to take home your coin. Carry it around in your pocket this week and let it remind you that everything you do is a choice you make. Think of your choices with the if-then idea in mind.**

Close in prayer.

BECOMING WISE: CHOICES

1. When you start making good_____ and put your childish ways behind you, you've entered into womanhood.

2. Often the hardest part of making a choice is not the actual_____ but_____ what you'll do.

3. With a partner answer these questions.

   A. What are some easy choices that you have every day?

      1.

      2.

      3.

      4.

   B. What are some hard choices that you have every day?

      1.

      2.

      3.

      4.

4. If you choose_____ to choose, you're still making a_____.

5. For the next few questions flip a coin to determine your future. If you get heads, that means YES. If you get tails, that means NO (unless H or T appears in the question).

   Good luck—your future depends on the answers!

   A. Will I get to be homecoming queen?_____

   B. Am I going to pass science this year?_____

   C. Will I totally humiliate myself at lunch tomorrow?_____

   D. Will I get married?_____

   E. Will I graduate from college?_____

   F. Will I have (H) two kids or (T) 10 kids?_____

   G. Am I going to have a dead-end job when I'm 30?_____

   H. Will I live in (H) a mansion or (T) a shack?_____

   I. Am I going to stab my friend in the back?_____

   J. Do I like pizza?_____

   K. Do I like the guy sitting closest to me in math?_____

   L. Should I start going by the nickname Oprah?_____

   M. Am I going to rob the lunch lady?_____

   N. Am I going to cheat on the next history exam?_____

6. A great deal of what_____ to us we cause directly or indirectly through our_____ (though there are exceptions, such as_____ or if your parents are _____).

7. Colossians 2:8 says, "Don't let _____ spoil your faith and joy with their philosophies, wrong and shallow answers based on men's thoughts and ideas, instead of on what Christ has said" (LB).

8. Isaiah 30:21 says, "Whether you turn to the right or to the left, your ears will hear a voice behind you saying, 'This is the way; _____.'"

9. By yourself circle the characteristics or choices that answer "Who do I want to be?"

Nice	Healthy	Musical
Rude	Peacemaker	Wise
Loving	Hard worker	Intelligent
Arrogant	Intolerant	Creative
Prideful	Racist	Addict
Liar	Exclusive	Gossiper
Godly	Taker	Thief
Honest	Thoughtful	Sweet
Selfish	Accepting	Bitter
Giving	Joyful	Angry
Humble	Patient	Vengeful
Bully	Faithful	Jealous
Annoying	Foolish	Ignorant
Athletic	Hateful	Fight for what is right
Popular	Leader	Self-controlled
Listener	Follower	Compassionate
Pure	Admirable	
Good student	Loyal	

10. How do I become that person?

    A. Determine priorities and_____.

    B. Set_____.

    C. Establish_____.

    D. _____ yourself for victories.

11. Determine priorities and values.

    What is a value? Webster tells us...

    A. Something you desire more when_____ to other things.

    B. Something you rate/think_____ of.

    C. What is VERY, VERY important to me?

BECOMING WISE: CHOICES

I'm so proud of you for all the work you're doing to help you grow in knowing yourself as well as becoming what God has created you to be!

Brainteaser

Here's a little riddle to get you thinking....

> Once there was a night watchman who'd been caught several times sleeping on the job. The boss issued an ultimatum that the watchman must not fall asleep ever again, but the very next night the watchman was caught again at his desk with his head in his hands, elbows resting on the desk. "Aha, I've caught you again," exclaimed the boss. The watchman's eyes popped open immediately, and he knew what had happened. Being a quick-thinking man, he said one word before looking up at the boss. The boss apologized profusely and went home.

What was the one word?_____

Soul Work questions

Now that you're thinking, go get a cola and your favorite snack, and let's get started. *HINT*: If you look back at your Reality Check sheet from class, it'll help you answer most of your Soul Work.

1. Have you ever made a really difficult choice? What was it?

2. You could say, "You sometimes learn from experiences, but you always learn from reflecting on those experiences." Reflect on a time you made a poor choice, one that wasn't so good for you. What can you learn from that experience?

3. Looking back at number nine on your **Reality Check** sheet, what can you say about the person you want to become?

4. Are there any other words you would like to add to the list?

5. Here's a brief list of some questions you should ask when discovering what you value.

   A. If my house were on fire, what would I grab while I was escaping?

   B. What do I want to accomplish with my day, year, schooling, career, family, life?

C. What things are important to me now? In the future?

D. What are things I won't give up?

E. Who do I want to be?

F. What are things I want to change about myself?

G. What do I need in any relationship?

H. What do I believe in?

I. Are there areas in my faith I won't compromise?

J. What am I really proud of about myself?

6. Using the characteristics you'd like to have (the items you circled in number nine on your Reality Check sheet) as well as the above questions (A-J), list the top five things you value. Remember, this is something you want to think about and ask God about.

A.

B.

C.

D.

E.

7. Ask your parents what they value. Write down their answers.

8. You're going to have a mini-interview with one of your grandparents. Even if this means you have to make a long-distance phone call, get permission to do it. If your grandparents are no longer alive, I'm very sorry to hear that. In that case, think of someone you know who's around grandparent age and ask them in your grandparents' honor.

A. What's one thing you would change in your life if you could go back in time?

B. We're talking about values. Did you ever have to work hard to accomplish something you value? (For example, in sports, marriage, schooling, work, parenting, etc.)

CHAPTER FOUR

BECOMING FOCUSED: SETTING GOALS

INGREDIENTS

Blindfold, peanut butter, jelly, bread, knife, hand drawing of a simple house, *Girl, Interrupted* DVD, *The Karate Kid* DVD, art supplies, printed-out pages of directions from your church to a far-off site from MapQuest or a similar map site (one page per girl in your group)

REVIEW SOUL WORK

Make sure they've each thought of at least one value. If they haven't, help them quickly brainstorm. Answer to the brainteaser: "Amen."

APPETIZER: BLINDFOLDED PB&J

Start today's session by selecting two volunteers. Blindfold one. The blindfolded girl will be giving directions to the other on how to make a peanut butter and jelly sandwich. The person making the sandwich can only do *exactly* what she's told. For example, if she's not told to take the bread out of the bag, when she's told to put peanut butter on the bread, she'll have to put it on the bag. You can give hints to the person following directions by asking things like, "Did she tell you to do that?"

Give these directions after you have your two volunteers: **You have two minutes to make a peanut butter and jelly sandwich. However, I'm of course going to give you a little twist. The one who's giving the directions will be blindfolded. The other person can ONLY do what your blindfolded partner tells you to do.**

If you have a couple of girls who think they can do this better than the first pair (and of course you will), let them try—but you need to mix it up again. This time have the blindfolded girl follow directions while standing in front of the girl giving the directions so it looks as if one person is the body and the other functions as the arms and hands.

If you're too chicken to try the PB&J, try this. Have one person draw a picture on the chalkboard or a piece of paper. The girl giving the directions isn't allowed to look at anything other than the paper you give her. Have her stand with her back to the person drawing. The paper you give the instructor should have a drawing of a very simple house with a door and a window or two. Your "instructor" is going to give directions to the other girl on how to draw this picture. Again, the person drawing can only do what she's told.

QUESTIONS AND COMMENTARY

Setting goals

Say, **Last week we decided one big thing that makes a girl become a woman is making good choices. Well, setting goals is one place where that happens.**

Now say, **If you're on a big trip to a destination you've never been to, you're going to need a map. If you don't think this is true, please tell me how to get to Denver, Iowa.** Pause...then say, **You can't do it because you've never been there. You need a map. Just like with making the PB&J or the picture, it would've really helped to have some well-thought-out plans or directions. One engineering class in some college actually did write out the directions for making a PB&J, and it turned out to be 13 pages long!**

Now say, **Often in our lives we forget we're even on a journey. We forget there's a map to follow because we've forgotten we have a destination. We forget about all the things we value just as Jenna did in last week's movie. As a result we no longer worry about what choices we're making because we've forgotten that our choices will have long-term effects.**

Specialty: Movie Clip

Show movie clip: *Girl, Interrupted* (from 1:12 "You know I have a problem" to 1:15 "For now"). After the clip ask, **What does Susanna realize in this clip?**

After you receive some answers, say, **She sees no one else is to blame for where she is, and she's the only one who's hindering her own future.**

Then say, **The choices we make do matter. At some point what we've chosen, good or bad, will catch up with us, and we'll have no one else to blame but ourselves. How can we prevent being our own biggest roadblock for our future?**

Next say, **Now that you spent some time last week figuring out some things you value, it's time to start working toward making those values a reality in your life. The way to get from where you are now to where you want to be and be sure you keep your values valuable is to use a map called "goals." Setting goals will guide you toward putting values into your life. Goals are your set of well-thought-out directions to get you the results you want. "I press on toward the goal to win the prize for which God has called me heavenward in Christ Jesus." (Philippians 3:14)**

Then say, **We've all set goals before. Some goals are set at the new year. What are some New Year's resolutions you've made before or ones you've heard others make?** After you receive some answers, say, **Some goals are set for us. What are some examples of these?** *(Possible answers: finish middle school, things parents tell you to accomplish)*

After some answers say, **One thing to learn before setting goals is about short-term and long-term gratification.** (You may need to explain what the word *gratification* means.) **We need to learn to tolerate frustration and control our impulses. What are some differences between long-term and short-term gratification?** After you receive some answers, tell your girls to fill in the blanks on questions one and two on their **Reality Check** sheets.

1. **Often what feels good <u>immediately</u> isn't what's good for us in the long run and is ultimately <u>destructive</u>. Can you think of an example?**

2. **Likewise what <u>hurts</u> or is hard right now is often the most <u>rewarding</u> in the future. Can you think of an example?**

Then say,

Reality Check

3. **Proverbs 14:12 affirms this idea: "There is a way that appears to be right...but in the end it leads to <u>death</u>."** (For the underlined word, multiple choices listed on their sheets are A. a really fun time, B. really mad parents, and C. death.)

Expand on the idea of how smoking, drinking, and drugs all seem pretty popular in middle school, high school, and college. However, they all lead to death—or at least unpleasant consequences.

Reality Check

6. A boundary helps you decide what you will and won't <u>accept</u> from others. It also determines what you will and won't <u>do</u>.

   Ask, **Aside from actual fences or boundaries in sports, can you think of an example of a boundary that determines limits?** *(Possible answer: I don't want my brother in my room. That's important to me. So when would I consider that my brother has crossed a line and decide to act in my defense? Maybe if I find something missing. I won't accept that, and I might choose to go talk to Mom and Dad.)*

   Now ask, **What would be a boundary that could end a friendship? What's something you wouldn't accept from a friend?**

After you receive some answers, ask, **Why do we set boundaries?**

Reality Check

7. 1 Corinthians 6:12 gives us one reason: "'I have the <u>right</u> to do anything,' you say—but not everything is <u>beneficial</u>. 'I have the right to do anything'—but I will not be mastered by anything."

   Say, **Think of it like this. You have this caterpillar. She's dark brown, hairy, and chubby and crawls on the ground dodging the feet of humans and animals. Every once in a while some seven-year-old boy picks her up, and she fears for her life, hoping she won't be fried in the sun under a magnifying glass. Well, she's spared from boys and one day goes into her cocoon. After enough time out comes a butterfly. This butterfly is beautiful. She has yellow, brown, black, and blue on her majestic wings. She's as free as a bird. People stop to watch her beauty as she flutters from one spot to the next. Do you think this butterfly is going to go back to her old ways? I guess she could crawl around on the ground and dodge feet, just hoping not to be caught or squashed. But why would she?**

   Now say, **Everything is *permissible* for me, but not everything is *beneficial*. You have total freedom to do what you think you'd like. But ask yourself, "Why would I?" Why be a caterpillar when you can be a butterfly?**

Reality Check

8. **Nothing will take away God's <u>love</u>; however, that doesn't mean a bad behavior has no consequences.** (For the underlined word, multiple choices listed on their sheets are A. sense of humor, B. love, and C. magic wand.)

    Say, **A girl who's drunk can choose to drive, but is that a beneficial choice? God will still love her if she kills someone on her way home; however, this wouldn't be good for her or the others involved. Can you think of similar examples?** Discuss their answers.

Reality Check

9. **We all have a center in our brain we'll call the "hate it but do it" center.**

    Explain, **This center is a place that takes our long-term goals and allows us to follow through with the hard work to accomplish those goals. It keeps us focused ahead.**

Specialty: Movie Clip

Show movie clip: *The Karate Kid* (from 1:15 "Daniel-san, come here" to 1:18 "Come back tomorrow.") Say, **Daniel is angry and ready to quit. He questions why he has to do all this tedious cleaning when what he wants to learn is karate. He later learns the cleaning is in fact helping him, and Daniel chooses to continue. What changes Daniel's attitude?**

After you receive some answers, say, **You have to think long term and do the hard work if you really want to see the results you hope for. Choosing a boundary is setting limits, rules, or standards for yourself. Setting and sticking to your boundaries often requires hard work, but not for nothing. Be the butterfly, not the caterpillar!**

Then say, **For example, a runner values running. Her goal is to place higher in the next meet than the meet before. Therefore, she now needs some boundaries or guidelines to make sure she accomplishes this goal. One boundary might be to run an extra half mile each day. Another might be to lift weights once a week to build more strength.**

Continue, **Let's try to set some sample boundaries together. I'll name a value and a goal associated with it; you name a boundary or guideline to help accomplish that goal.** (Leader Note: *The responses don't have to be exact matches to those given in italics.*)

Value: playing piano

Goal: to get to the next level book in six months

Boundary: *(practice 30 minutes a day)*

Value: getting good grades

Goal: to get an A on the next test

Boundary: *(study for 20 minutes each night on that subject)*

Reality Check

10. **With your partners choose one boundary for the value and goal you set earlier.**

After some time, say

Reality Check

11. <u>Rewards</u> **are what keep you going.**

Say, **We all need rewards. Some rewards are given by other people. Some rewards you need to make sure you give to yourself. The reward for the runner may be the medal she receives when she places. It may also be something she gives herself—perhaps a day off.**

Use the previous values, goals, and boundaries to come up with rewards—use the same call-and-response format as before.

Value: playing piano

Goal: to get to the next level book in six months

Boundary: practice 30 minutes a day

Reward: *(When I reach the next level, I'll get a new book to play just for fun.)*

Value: getting good grades

Goal: to get an A on the next test

Boundary: study for 20 minutes each night on that subject

Reward: *(When I get an A on the next test, I'll have a friend spend the night.)*

Reality Check

12. **With your partners set one reward to go with your value, goal, and boundary.**

Specialty: Comic Strip (Option)

Say, **Using the paper, crayons, pencils, or markers provided, create a comic strip showing the value, goal, boundary, and reward you've been working on.** Let them know how long they have left. If you're out of time, you could add this to their **Soul Work** to do with any one of their goal sets.

TAKE OUT

Say, **We can all make a PB&J without 13 pages of directions. However, not all of life is that easy. Goals show us where we want to go.** (Have on hand several copies of printed-out directions from your church to a far-off destination such as Denver, Iowa, from MapQuest or some other map site.) Give each girl a map to remind her she needs to think about where she's going and make choices that'll get her there.

Close by saying, **Boundaries let us know what will and won't help us get to our goal. And rewards keep us looking ahead and make ourselves feel good about a job well done. No one can make good choices for us. That's up to you. This is your life—are you who you want to be?**

REALITY CHECK

BECOMING FOCUSED: SETTING GOALS

"I press on toward the goal to win the prize for which God has called me heavenward in Christ Jesus." (Philippians 3:14)

1. Often what feels good_____ isn't what's good for us in the long run and is ultimately_____. Can you think of an example?

2. Likewise what_____ or is hard right now is often the most_____ in the future. Can you think of an example?

3. Proverbs 14:12 affirms this idea: "There is a way that appears to be right...but in the end it leads to_____."

   A a really fun time.

   B. really mad parents.

   C. death.

4. You need to think_____ gratification when setting goals.

5. With one or two partners share one value on your list from last week's Soul Work and help each other set a good_____. (You only need to write down your own.)

6. A boundary helps you decide what you will and won't_____ from others. It also determines what you will and won't_____.

7. 1 Corinthians 6:12 gives us one reason: "'I have the_____ to do anything,' you say—but not everything is_____. 'I have the right to do anything'—but I will not be mastered by anything."

8. Nothing will take away God's_____; however, that doesn't mean a bad behavior has no consequences.

   A. sense of humor

   B. love

   C. magic wand

9. We all have a center in our brain we'll call the "_____" center.

10. With your partners choose one boundary for the value and goal you set earlier. (Only write yours.)

11. _____ are what keep you going.

12. With your partners set one reward to go with your value, goal, and boundary. (Only write yours.)

BECOMING FOCUSED: SETTING GOALS

I'm so proud of how well you're doing. Keep working hard and you'll see God helping you become who God intends for you to be. In turn you will be becoming of Christ.

Brainteaser

These can be tough, so don't be afraid to ask your parents for their thoughts!

1. F FAR E FAR W_____
2. SSSSSSSSSS C_____
3. EZ

    I I _____
4. YOUR HAT

    KEEP IT _____
5. DATE DATE_____

Soul Work questions

You're going to work the next few days on setting a goal, boundary, and reward for the other four values (since you did one of your five during the lesson) from last week's **Soul Work** (question six). If you didn't finish choosing five values for last week's **Soul Work**, do that first. If you said you value your family, you might have a hard time setting goals and boundaries for that. Consider revising it to "I value being a good sister or daughter" or "I value having a good relationship with my parents." Try to make long-term goals, but also allow for short-term rewards. Think back to the end of our lesson for help. We talked about several examples like this one.

> **Value: getting good grades**
>
> **Goal: to get an A on the next test**
>
> **Boundary: study for 20 minutes each night on that subject**
>
> **Reward:** *(When I get an A on the next test, I'll have a friend spend the night.)*

Also be sure to record when you reach a goal or get your reward. You can use the back of this page if you need more room.

Here are some other questions to get you thinking. Answer questions one through four for each of the four values you didn't work on during class time.

1. What do I want to work on, improve, or change in my schoolwork, extracurricular activities, relationships, character, or another area? (value)

2. What's the result I want? (goal)

3. What do I need to do to get there? (boundary)

4. What will help me think long term? What will keep me focused and be a good reward for all my hard work? (reward)

5. Ask someone who might have something to do with this value, goal, boundary, and reward set (coach, teacher, parent, etc.) to look at these things and help you determine whether you're thinking long term and whether you've chosen appropriate goals, boundaries, and rewards.

Ask yourself each day, "Are the choices I'm making helping me reach my goals?"

"Are these choices staying within my boundaries?"

CHAPTER FIVE

BECOMING SPLENDOROUS: ACCEPTING THE SKIN YOU'RE IN

INGREDIENTS

Homemade carnival mirror, paper and crayons, Kendall Payne's CD *Jordan's Sister* and printed-out lyrics to the song "Supermodels" from the CD, Steven Curtis Chapman's CD *Speechless* and printed-out lyrics to the song "Fingerprints of God" from the CD, *Austin Powers in Goldmember* DVD, bubble gum, one small bag of the greasiest potato chips you know of, fingerprinting ink

REVIEW SOUL WORK

Answers to the brainteaser—

1. Few and far between

2. Tennessee

3. Easy on the eyes

4. Keep it under your hat

5. Double date

Leader Note: *Try to make a carnival mirror—like the ones that make you look taller or shorter or fatter or thinner. If you're ahead of the game, go online to www.carnivalmirror.com. You can buy the mirror material for about $5 and just put it on the wall. It's great! But it will take a couple weeks to arrive. The other option is to go to a floral shop and get some mylar, which is sold from a roll. It's pretty cheap. (However, it's very frustrating to work with.) Place the carnival mirror so everyone can see it when they enter the room. You'll use this mirror later in the lesson.*

APPETIZER: CRAYON PORTRAITS

Say, **Today we're going to start by testing your artistic skills. Find a partner and grab a piece of paper each and some crayons. I want you to draw the best portrait of your partner that you can.** Give them three to five minutes (or the length of one song of your choice). Let them know ahead of time that their last names aren't da Vinci or Rembrandt, so they don't have a long time. When the portraits are done,

Say, **Yet it seems so hard to say no at times. When you're thinking about the long term, these are obvious things to avoid. But we all forget we're on this journey for life, and we forget to think about where our choices will put us in 10 or 20 years. Or sometimes even where they'll put us when we get home!**

Now say, **Remember the fuzzy photos I showed you a few weeks ago? What was the point of those? It's important to remember there's a bigger picture out there. When we set a goal for ourselves, it keeps us looking at that big picture instead of everything happening around us every minute.**

Reality Check

4. **You need to think <u>long-term</u> gratification when setting goals.**

   Say, **Let's look at examples of some things we may value. What would be the difference between short-term and long-term thinking in these cases?**

   If you value playing piano, a good goal may be...

   If you value getting good grades, your goal may be...

   If you value sexual purity, your goal may be...

Reality Check

5. **With one or two partners share one value on your list from last week's Soul Work and help each other set a good <u>goal</u>.**

Boundaries

After the girls have had some time to set good goals, ask, **What's a boundary?** After you receive some answers, say, **A boundary is a line that marks a limit. Every backyard has a boundary. In sports, boundary lines show where the ball goes out of bounds and ends the play. But boundaries can also mean limits in our personal lives.**

have the partners turn the portraits in to you. Mix them up and let the girls guess who is who. Some possible questions to ask—**Who made the portrait that looks most like the real person? Do any of them look identical? What are some funny things on the pictures?**

After the discussion say, **Today we're talking about being content with our looks and accepting the skin we're in. But it can be really hard to do.**

QUESTIONS AND COMMENTARY

Ask, **If you could be anyone else, who would you be? Why?** After some answers ask, **If you could change one thing during your whole last year of life what would it be?**

After receiving some answers, say, **Isn't it funny that the one thing we would change about our lives rarely has anything to do with our appearance, yet our appearance is what we're consumed with every day? In fact, many people, if they could be anyone else in the world, would be someone good-looking—how many of us thought the same thing?**

Say, **You have to be able to overcome three major hurdles to accept your appearance.**

Reality Check

1. **Stop <u>comparing</u> yourself to others.**

Specialty: Quiz

Have the girls fill out the quiz on their **Reality Check** sheets.

How often do you...

(never = 1; every moment I breathe = 5)

_____ Give other girls the once-over?

_____ Wish you looked like someone else?

_____ Look at a magazine and feel depressed because you'll never look like that?

_____ Change outfits in the morning because the one you just tried on looks bad on you?

_____ Give a girl the cold shoulder because she looks better than you?

_____ Think to yourself, "How did *that* girl get *that* guy?"

_____ Worry you'll never attract the guy you like?

_____ Spend more than one hour getting ready in the morning?

_____ Check your mirror before going into school or stores?

_____ Check every mirror you pass?

_____ Reapply makeup or redo your hair?

Say, **If you scored more than 20 on this, you may want to evaluate whether you're struggling with comparing yourself to others.**

Continue, **We look around the room and figure out what we're not wearing or looking like that we *obviously* are supposed to be. This goes beyond our clothes. We compare our waists, thighs, breasts, eyes, smiles, noses, nails, and everything else. We think, "I may have beautiful eyes, but she's skinnier. My hair may be incredible, but she has a chest to die for."**

Reality Check

A. Our opinions of our bodies change according to who we're <u>comparing</u> ourselves to that day.

Say, **Remember, only eight women in three billion look perfect. Find a partner sitting three people to your left and discuss the questions in B on your outlines.**

Reality Check

B. What happens when we get caught up in comparing ourselves to others all the time? How are we going to feel about ourselves? Where's our focus? Where do we find happiness if we're always failing?

Specialty: Supermodels

Play the song "Supermodels" by Kendall Payne from her CD *Jordan's Sister*. This is an upbeat, hip-hop-style, humorous song about how we'll never measure up to looking like supermodels. (Find the lyrics on the Internet and print them out for your girls to follow during the song.)

After the song say, **You're comparing yourself to someone who has nothing to do with you. It's ridiculous to try to look like everyone else. We can try, but we'll never succeed. What would you think about a cat who went around all day moaning about how she wants to look like a dog? Or how about a turtle who wants to look like a giraffe? You're not anyone else. Your body is different.**

Reality Check

C. Accepting, loving, and being content with how God made us isn't always <u>easy</u>. Nor does it come naturally. It's a <u>choice</u>. Sometimes it's an hourly choice. You can't change <u>what you look like</u> for the most part. Put stock in who you are in your <u>heart</u>—God does. Besides, that's who you end up being anyway.

Specialty: Fingerprints of God

Say, **One day your best friend comes to you in tears because she feels so horrible about herself. Her boyfriend has broken up with her, and she's just sure it's because of Abby, who is sooooo much prettier than her. She's sure no guy will ever think she's pretty or like her.**

Ask, **What would you tell her? Write a quick note that you'd pass her when you see her in the hall.** Have the girls write these on the back of the page of lyrics to Steven Curtis Chapman's "Fingerprints of God." (Find the lyrics on the Internet and print them out for your girls to follow during the song when you play it later.) Have them keep these notes for later. Allow each girl to share her note if she'd like.

Reality Check

D. Psalm 139:13-16 says, "For you created my inmost being; you knit me together in my mother's womb. I praise you because I am fearfully and wonderfully made; your works are wonderful, I know that full well. My frame was not hidden from you when I was made in the secret place. When I was woven together in the depths of the earth, your eyes saw my unformed body."

Have the girls underline "My frame was not hidden from you" on their Reality Check outlines.

Ask, **When you compare yourself to others, what does that communicate to God, who created you?**

After you receive some answers, say, **This verse says God knew you in the womb and did everything according to a divine plan for you. So hurdle number one is to stop comparing yourself to others. Hurdle number two...**

Reality Check

2. **Stop worrying about others' <u>opinions</u>.**

Specialty: Movie Clip

Show movie clip: *Austin Powers in Goldmember* (chapter 6, or 39:01: "Aww, Basil. What's happening?" to 40:43: "Molay Moley," this clip is about how Austin can't stop staring at a guy's mole.)

After the clip say, **I think we've all felt this way about some part of us. We feel as if someone's staring at some part of our body and as if it's all they can focus on. We then walk away not being able to see anything else, either. Too often we let others dictate how we feel about ourselves.**

Reality Check

A. **The day we discover we aren't beautiful as the world defines beauty can be a <u>devastating</u> day.**

Share about a time in your life when you really felt like this or something about your body that makes you feel inadequate. The girls won't want to share if no one else has shared. Ask, **Does anyone have a time you'd share about when someone made you feel bad about your body?**

Reality Check

B. When someone (even if it's yourself) makes you feel less than beautiful, you must make a choice and <u>decide</u> that what was said about you isn't true.

Say, **Philippians 4:8 tells us to set our minds on things that are true. Only then will we be able to let go, and the truth will set us free from the stronghold the lie has on us. We won't automatically remember this. But as we choose to remember, it'll come more and more naturally to us.** Take this opportunity to affirm each girl who shared an example, saying to each, **It isn't true.**

Now say, **Get out those portraits you drew of each other. How would you feel if you really looked this way? Obviously, these are just for fun, and we never intended these to be real portraits of each other. However, when we care about what others think of us, it's just as if we take these pictures and say we really look this way.**

Continue with, **We have many people who "paint pictures" of how we look—ugly, fat, sloppy, out of style—and instead of questioning their opinions, we believe we do look that way. That's as crazy as believing these pictures accurately represent what we truly look like.**

Tell this story: **Lisa Ryan was once Miss California. In her book *For Such a Time as This*, she tells of the time when she was about to give away her crown at the end of her year. Listen to her story about the choice she made. "I am ashamed to admit that it happened to me, but it did. When I was about to give up my crown as Miss California, a gown was specially designed for my final walk down the runway. When the producer of the show saw it, he said that it wasn't sexy enough. The television broadcast needed higher ratings, and he suggested that it was time for me to shed my 'good girl' image. He wanted the cleavage cut to the waist and the slit of the skirt to the top of my thigh."**

Say, **Discuss with a partner how you would've responded— not what the right response would be, but how *you* would've responded.**

After a minute say, **Here's the rest of the story: "I was uncomfortable with his suggestions, but I was a people pleaser. I didn't value myself enough or have the confidence to say no. So the designer made the changes. To be honest, I was a little intrigued by the attention and sense of power it gave me. I still remember that final walk. The dress was a showstopper, all right, but I had crossed a line, and I knew it. I was a professing Christian, and that dress didn't portray the elegance and integrity I wanted to be remembered for. In that instance and others like it, I compromised my character."**[1]

Reality Check

C. When your <u>looks</u> are more important than showing God's <u>love</u> to others, you've made an <u>idol</u> for yourself.

Specialty: Greasy Chips

You need a couple of girls to volunteer for this competition. Each girl needs one piece of gum and one small baggie of the greasiest chips you can find. (I won't insult any particular brand by naming it in a book but you know what I mean. I'm talking about the ones that sit in the bag, and you can see the oil dripping from your cart on the way to the checkout.) The competition's goal is to be the first one to eat all the chips, then blow a bubble with the gum. If the game is starting to go awhile, you can speed it up by telling them to stop eating any more chips or no one wins because no one can blow a bubble.

Ask, **Why was it hard to blow a bubble?** Wait for some answers, then say, **Because salt and grease don't mix well with sugar. This makes it very difficult to blow a bubble. Have you ever seen someone try to mix water with oil? They won't mix. You can shake up the combination and think it's mixed, but within a minute or so it all separates again.**

Reality Check

D. Matthew 6:24 tells us, "No one can serve two masters. Either you will hate the one and love the other, or you will be devoted to the one and despise the other."

[1] Lisa Ryan, *For Such a Time As This* (Multnomah Publishers, Inc. 2001), 26.

Tell the girls, **Circle the words** *two masters* **on your outlines. You choose one or the other. Our choice to care about what others think of us and our desire to care about what God thinks can't mix. It's fine to look stylish and smell good, but when you compare yourself to everyone around you and care what they think, then you stop caring about what God thinks.**

Now say, **Everyone had an opinion about Jesus. They weren't afraid to let him know what they thought. Isaiah 53:3 says, "He was despised and rejected by others, a man of suffering, and familiar with pain. Like one from whom people hide their faces he was despised, and we held him in low esteem." People spit on him; they yelled at him—you name it. All he had to do was say, "Forget it; I quit! This is too hard and people are too mean. I want them to like me. Their opinions matter more to me than yours, God." And it would've been finished.**

Continue, **Philippians 2:5-11 tells us what we're supposed to do:**

> **In your relationships with one another, have the same attitude of mind Christ Jesus had: Who, being in very nature God, did not consider equality with God something to be used to his own advantage; rather, he made himself nothing by taking the very nature of a servant, being made in human likeness. And being found in appearance as a human being, he humbled himself by becoming obedient to death—even death on a cross! Therefore God exalted him to the highest place and gave him the name that is above every name, that at the name of Jesus every knee should bow, in heaven and on earth and under the earth, and every tongue acknowledge that Jesus Christ is Lord, to the glory of God the Father.**

Say, **God wants you to be happy about what you look like. God wants you to look your best. God wants you to have fun wearing makeup and doing your hair. It just needs to be less important than loving God and doing what God wants you to do. After all...**

Reality Check

E. Beauty was God's idea.

Ask, **What are some examples of God's beauty in creation?** After you get some answers, say, **And remember...*you*! You are a creation of God. God's proud of the work it took to create you. Your beauty is a gift from God.**

If you can, tell a story about a girl from your school days who may not have been the prettiest but was nice to everyone, was well regarded, and in the end, got to be homecoming queen or something similar.

Reality Check

3. Start relying on your splendor to make you beautiful.

Ask, **Have you ever seen those crazy funhouse carnival mirrors? What are they like? What do they do?** If you were able to make a mirror, let the girls take turns looking into it. Now say, **They distort your true reflection and make you look way different. This is what our culture—could be the media, people at school, people at home, yourself—does to you. But when someone tells you you're ugly, fat, too short, too tall, too this, or too that, then...**

Reality Check

A. You look in a mirror and see yourself as what everyone's opinions are even though you aren't any of those things.

Say, **You start to see yourself as ugly, fat, too short, too tall, too this, or too that. You get to a point where you can no longer see a reflection of the person God made. That person is still there and still just as valuable, but you can't see her because you're blinded by all those other opinions. Sometimes we're hardest on ourselves. We see the worst in ourselves. The reflection is distorted. It doesn't mean what you see is true or real—it means the reflection is wrong. But it's all you can see.**

Reality Check

B. What we see in any mirror is never a true <u>reflection</u>. Others' opinions change what we see, and what we see is a reflection of how we <u>feel</u> about ourselves.

C. Proverbs 31:30 says, "Charm is deceptive, and beauty is fleeting; but a woman who fears the LORD is to be praised." What does this mean?

Have some of them share their answers. Then add, **Do you know what happens when you get old? You get old! Even though some of the older Miss Americas are still pretty for their age, they could never compete with the beauty of the younger candidates.**

Ask, **What are some things that can change your appearance?** After you receive a few answers, say, **If you have an accident, it can alter the way you look. You may get a visible scar, or a fire could leave you not resembling anything you looked like before. We must get to a place where we can value more than our bodies. What happens to you when your looks go out the window? How will that leave you feeling about yourself?**

Reality Check

D. Ezekiel 16:14 says, "And your fame spread among the nations on account of your beauty, because the <u>splendor</u> I had given you made your beauty perfect declares the Sovereign LORD."

Ask, **What's the difference between beauty and splendor? Beauty is surface level; splendor is the magnificence of your being, often in reference to your reputation. Think of diamonds. They're pretty. However, if you get them under the right light and hold them up against some black velvet, they're radiant. The diamonds didn't change, but what you did with the diamonds changed everything. Your outward appearance is fine, but your splendor (inner qualities and what you do with yourself) makes your outward beauty perfect.**

Say, **The Ezekiel verse is talking about Jerusalem, but it can be applied to us, too.**

Reality Check

E. <u>God</u> gave you your beauty, and the beauty God gave you on the inside, your splendor, makes your outer beauty even greater.

Say, **Listen to this passage from 1 Peter 3:3-5:**

> **Your beauty should not come from outward adornment, such as elaborate hairstyles and the wearing of gold jewelry and fine clothes. Rather, it should be that of your inner self, the unfading beauty of a gentle and quiet spirit, which is of great worth in God's sight. For this is the way the holy women of the past who put their hope in God used to make themselves beautiful.** (NIV)

Share about someone you knew growing up who you thought then was incredibly beautiful, but now you see that it was her inner beauty you were reacting to.

Next say, **Without naming names, think of someone you don't like. How pretty is she? Do any of you dislike someone you also consider pretty?**

After receiving some answers, say, **It's hard to see beauty outside when there's not much beauty showing from the inside.**

Offer a personal example in the most godly, loving way possible. Finish by saying, **God created you. Every bit of you. There's really nothing you can do to change that. You need to accept how God formed you and let your inside make you beautiful on the outside.**

Specialty: Fingerprints of God (Reprise)

Play the song "Fingerprints of God" by Steven Curtis Chapman. Let the girls follow the lyrics on their printouts while they listen to the song.

TAKE OUT

After the song's over, say, **Remember the note you wrote to your friend on the back of the song lyrics? I want you to put that note somewhere and let it be a letter to yourself for when you are feeling down. Read it when you're getting caught up in comparing yourself to others and worrying about their opinions. Remember—God made you. God knows exactly what you're supposed to look like. We need to embrace who we are and start relying on our splendor.**

Have each girl put a fingerprint on her note. Challenge the girls to put the notes on their mirrors at home as reminders that they're beautiful because God made them.

REALITY CHECK

BECOMING SPLENDOROUS: ACCEPTING THE SKIN YOU'RE IN

1. Stop_____ yourself to others.

   How often do you...

   (never=1; every moment I breathe=5)

   _____ Give other girls the once-over?

   _____ Wish you looked like someone else?

   _____ Look at a magazine and feel depressed because you'll never look like that?

   _____ Change outfits in the morning because the one you just tried on looks bad on you?

   _____ Give a girl the cold shoulder because she looks better than you?

   _____ Think to yourself, "How did *that* girl get *that* guy?"

   _____ Worry you'll never attract the guy you like?

   _____ Spend more than one hour getting ready in the morning?

   _____ Check your mirror before going into school or stores?

   _____ Check every mirror you pass?

   _____ Reapply makeup or redo your hair?

   A. Our opinions of our bodies change according to who we're_____ ourselves to that day.

   B. What happens when we get caught up in comparing ourselves to others all the time? How are we going to feel about ourselves? Where's our focus? Where do we find happiness if we're always failing?

   C. Accepting, loving, and being content with how God made us isn't always_____.
   Nor does it come naturally. It's a_____. Sometimes it's an hourly choice.
   You can't change _____
   for the most part. Put stock in who you are in your_____—God does. Besides,
   that's who you end up being anyway.

D. Psalm 139:13-16 says, "For you created my inmost being; you knit me together in my mother's womb. I praise you because I am fearfully and wonderfully made; your works are wonderful, I know that full well. My frame was not hidden from you when I was made in the secret place. When I was woven together in the depths of the earth, your eyes saw my unformed body."

2. Stop worrying about others'_____.

A. The day we discover we aren't beautiful as the world defines beauty can be a_____ day.

B. When someone (even if it's yourself) makes you feel less than beautiful, you must make a choice and_____ that what was said about you isn't true.

C. When your_____ are more important than showing God's_____ to others, you've made an_____ for yourself.

D. Matthew 6:24 tells us, "No one can serve two masters. Either you will hate the one and love the other, or you will be devoted to the one and despise the other."

E. _____ was God's idea.

3. Start relying on your_____ to make you beautiful.

A. You look in a mirror and see yourself as what everyone's_____ are even though you aren't any of those things.

B. What we see in any mirror is never a true_____. Others' opinions change what we see, and what we see is a reflection of how we_____ about ourselves.

C. Proverbs 31:30 says "Charm is deceptive, and beauty is fleeting; but a woman who fears the LORD is to be praised." What does this mean?

D. Ezekiel 16:14 says, "And your fame spread among the nations on account of your beauty, because the_____ I had given you made your beauty perfect declares the Sovereign LORD."

E. _____ gave you your beauty, and the beauty God gave you on the inside, your splendor, makes your outer beauty even greater.

BECOMING SPLENDOROUS: ACCEPTING THE SKIN YOU'RE IN

Brainteaser

Tell me what these statements mean.

1. Girl Guys Guys _____

2. L E G A L _____

3. $1,000,000 Girl _____

4. Far _____ _____ _____ _____ _____ Home _____

5. Gnikool _____

Okay, circle the answer that applies to you after doing the brainteaser:

A. I've used all my energy and brainpower up and can't possibly go on.

B. You've really made me mad, and I can't think about anything serious when I have these brainteasers hanging over my head.

C. I'm way too smart for you—what else do you have for me?

All right, all right, enough craziness! Grab your favorite pen and let's get on with things.

Soul Work questions

1. On a scale of 1-5 (1 = not me at all; 5 = how I feel most of the time) rate how you feel in these situations.

   A. Some days I feel so ugly I wish I could stay home so I wouldn't have to see anyone._____

   B. Some days I feel as if I'll never grow out of this little-kid look and be beautiful._____

   C. When I choose clothes, I think more about what others would like than what I like._____

   D. When I don't like how I look, I often avoid talking with other people._____

E. If it's time to leave the house and I haven't had time to finish getting ready, I'd rather be late and finish getting ready than be on time and not be ready._____

2. What does this tell you about how you feel about your body? Do you rely on your looks more than your inner self?

3. Write about a time you were embarrassed or ashamed about your body.

4. Regarding question three, were you embarrassed/ashamed because you were: (circle all that apply)

    A. comparing yourself to others

    B. worrying about others' opinions

    C. relying on your outward appearance instead of your inner splendor to make you beautiful

5. How are carnival mirrors like others' opinions of us?

6. What's the one thing you like least about your body? Did some situation or event make you feel this way?

7. What do you love about your body?

8. Why do you care about what others think of your appearance?

9. 1 Samuel 16:7 says, "The LORD does not look at the things human beings look at. People look at the outward appearance, but the Lord looks at the heart." What's God's point?

10. We decided in class that it isn't bad to spend time on your appearance. However, you need a balance. How do you know when you've turned your appearance into an idol— something more important than God or showing God's love?

11. Remember your hero we talked about in an earlier lesson? This is a person you know personally who you respect and would love to be like someday. Give that person a call this week and ask her how she deals with not liking her body sometimes. Ask her who she thinks is the most radiant person she actually knows (not on TV) and why. Ask her to pray for you to have the courage to accept and become content with the skin you're in. Write down her answers to your questions.

CHAPTER SIX

BECOMING BALANCED: KEEPING YOUR BODY IN CHECK

INGREDIENTS

Masking tape or sticky labels for game, paper and pens for each girl, fairy tale books, *Legally Blonde* DVD, two larger matching wrapped presents, several small gifts wrapped in wedding paper (one for each girl in your group)

REVIEW SOUL WORK

Here are the answers to the brainteasers.

1. Two guys after one girl
2. Legal spaced
3. Million-dollar girl
4. Far away from home
5. Looking backward

Say, **Last week we talked about being content with your body. Don't worry about what you look like on the outside. Let's see where this and some other ideas came from about who women are supposed to be.**

APPETIZER: SUPERHERO LABELS

Write the names of some superheroes on masking tape or on labels. These can be good guys and bad guys. Each student will have one name placed on her back. The object of this game is for the girls to write down as many names as they can that are on each others' backs. They can use the wall or any object to cover up the names on their backs. But they can't use their hands or their papers to cover the names up. Pass out paper and pens and have your girls play the game; the first to write down all the names wins and gets a round of applause.

Say, **As little girls we start dreaming about our weddings. Why does this start at such a young age? Let's look at some fairy tales**

we grew up hearing. If you happen to have these books at home, bring them in as visuals. Summarize the fairy tales, saying things like:

Cinderella—she's treated horribly by her stepfamily, but one evening at a ball the prince thinks she's pretty—and then her life is forever happy.

Snow White—her beauty is too much for her stepmom, so she tries to have Snow White killed. Instead Snow White falls into a deep sleep and is in waiting until a man wants her and kisses her. Then she can live happily ever after.

Sleeping Beauty—same with her. She's left helpless, at the mercy of a man to decide whether she's pretty enough to fall in love with (by merely looking at her), and then she can live happily ever after.

The Little Mermaid—she's so obsessed with one man's looks— and his alone—that she risks her soul to have one chance to be with him. She spends the next few days desperate for this guy to like her even though they've never met before. If he accepts her, she too can live happily ever after.

Then say, **All the women are supposed to be rescued by their princes and live happily ever after. Their lives aren't fulfilled until the day they're accepted and loved by the men who then make their lives happy—men they hardly knew, if they even knew them at all before.**

Explain, **This idea doesn't end when we're no longer little girls. We're bombarded by the idea that as females we're not complete until we have men at our sides. You find the idea on billboards, in movies, on TV, in magazines, in books, at school, even at home sometimes. No wonder you have a hard time and think something's wrong with you if you don't have a boyfriend or "no one likes" you. Remember the collages we made? By the looks of those, this idea seems true.**

Next say, **But the news isn't all bad. We may not be whole and happy until we have men, but evidently, we're also not left helpless. Women have a power over men—at least our culture teaches us we have one particular power. See if you can figure out this secret power.**

Continue, **Let's look again at our fairy tales:**

Cinderella—the prince isn't at all interested in any woman until the mere sight of Cinderella, and then poof—he doesn't even need to know her name to know he wants to marry her. He searches all night and won't stop until he finds her.

Snow White—the prince never even met the girl, but his kiss of true love breaks the spell on her, and they live happily ever after.

Sleeping Beauty—they met once, and that's all it took for her to woo her man.

The Little Mermaid—interestingly, this prince takes the time to get to know Ariel, yet when one other woman comes along, all seems to be over for Ariel.

QUESTIONS AND COMMENTARY

Then say, **In our game the names we were trying to guess on each other's backs all have at least one superpower. Some have powers they use for good and some for evil. You all have a superpower, too. What do you think this secret power is?**

Reality Check

1. **Your superpower is called "sex appeal."**

   Ask, **What is sex appeal?** Once you get some answers, ask, **Why does it work?** After some answers say, **The superheroes in our opening game all use superpowers, some for good and some for evil. How do you think sex appeal is used?**

   After you get some answers, say, **It isn't just fairy tales that teach this. Our culture teaches that women are sex objects because sex appeal is what gets men's attention. And if we can get their attention, we too can live "happily ever after."**

Specialty: Movie Clip

Now show the movie clip: *Legally Blonde* (chapter 20—the girls are all in the beauty salon, and Elle is teaching them how to get a guy's attention: "Bend and snap!") Say, **This is an example of what our culture calls "sex appeal." Now ask yourself...What are people going to notice** about you? What kind of person do others think you are? Is that what you want?

Then say, **As adolescent girls, you have no idea how much power you have. All you know is that certain clothing and actions get you attention. But boys and girls are very different.**

Reality Check

2. **Each gender has one of the five <u>senses</u> that's stronger than the <u>other gender's</u>.**

   A. Females tend to have a stronger sense of <u>smell</u>.

   Say, **It isn't that we smell things better than males do; rather, smell often influences us more than it does guys. Can you give some examples?**

   After you get some answers, say, **Likewise**...

Reality Check

   B. <u>Vision</u> tends to be a stronger sense for guys.

   Continue with, **Again, guys aren't able to see farther and better than women; rather, sight influences them more than their other senses do. Can you give some examples?**

   After you receive some answers, say, **That's why the superpower called sex appeal works on men. They're influenced by what they see. Many women act the way they do because it gets them attention.**

Specialty: Presents

Now grab your two larger presents. They should be two same-sized packages wrapped exactly the same way. You can wrap empty boxes as long as you make them the same size with the same paper. Using wedding wrapping paper would be a bonus. Ask the girls which gift they'd pick if they could have only one. Now tear a section of paper off one gift and ask, **If you came in on Christmas morning and saw both of these under the tree, which one would get *noticed* first, and which one would get more attention?** We'll talk more about this later and about which one they'd pick, etc.

For now say, **As with these presents, if you take off some of your wrapping (clothes), you'll get some attention. I'm not going to lie to you. If you show enough skin, talk a certain way, and act a certain way, guys will notice you.**

Then say, **Let's take a little quiz.** Have the girls fill in the blanks on their **Reality Check** outlines as to how many of each category they see in a given day.

3. In a given day I see...

_____ cleavage

_____ panty edges sticking out of pants

_____ belly buttons

_____ bra straps

_____ skin showing below the belly button

Say, **It's not just about looking cute and fashionable; it all comes back to those boys.**

Then say, **Remember when we talked about boys being totally visually stimulated? Another way to say it is that the things boys do and the things they think about are motivated by what they see. In fact, if you show a little cleavage, boys' minds fill in the rest they can't see. You show your belly button, and they imagine the rest. It's an unintentional invitation.**

Maybe you're thinking, **"But who cares? That's their problem! I'm just trying to be cute and trendy. Everyone looks like this. I can't be held responsible for what guys do and think. Right?"**

Answer by saying, **Well, yes and no. It's totally boys' responsibility to be godly and control themselves. Only they can choose to be transformed into the mind of Christ. Totally not your problem. Hopefully, boys are trying to become more like Christ every day. But on the other hand, guys are used to seeing women as sex objects. Remember all the stuff we're learning about the media and what they want you to believe? All the stuff our culture is lying to you about, it's lying to boys about, too. They're being trained just as you are.**

Reality Check

4. To boys you're a walking <u>billboard</u>.

Ask, **What are billboards used for?** After you get some responses, say, **They advertise. You use advertising for yourself, too—what you wear reflects what you want to sell about yourself. Most boys think that what you show them in public is nothing compared to what you'll show in private. So if you advertise your bra strap in public for anyone to see, then you're probably selling the idea that you'd show at least the whole bra in private. If you advertise your panty strap in public, you're probably selling the idea that you'll show the whole panties in private. If you advertise your cleavage in public, you're probably selling the idea that you'll show your whole breast in private.**

Say, **Maybe some of you are fine with that because it gets boys' attention, which feels good—and besides, you aren't going to let them "buy" what you're "selling." But remember where guys' minds often go? Let's say you like a new guy in school. You're trying to get his attention with your looks. My bet is, you're getting it. But do you have any idea who else you're attracting? Say one day you and your best friend are walking in the mall when you pass by Grandpa John on a bench waiting for Grandma Betty. When you walk by in your short skirt and your tight shirt that shows your tummy, guess who you're attracting now? Grandpa John just followed your cleavage line and filled in all the missing pieces. He just checked out your billboard, saw what was for sale, and went shopping in his mind. That's right—you just gave Grandpa your ad. Gross! What about when you go to your best friend's house? What are you inviting her dad or her brothers to check out?**

Modesty

Say, **The word *modesty* has gotten lost and misunderstood these days. Most people hear the word *modest* and think of old-fashioned dress. That's not the case. What does the word *modest* mean?**

After you get some answers, say...

Reality Check

5. **Modesty is looking normal without drawing <u>attention</u> to yourself.**

Say, **That's pretty good. Modesty is also about protecting yourself from men and boys who aren't choosing to be godly.**

Continue, **Look again at these presents. What's the difference between them? After you get some answers, say, One's torn. We decided earlier that if the torn one was under the Christmas tree, it'd get the most attention—just as when girls wear little clothing, they get more attention than girls who wear a normal amount of clothing. But which gift would you pick if you were only allowed to open one present? Why?**

After you receive some answers, say, **You're a precious gift. For some reason our culture tells us you have more value if you take a little bit of clothing off here and here and here. Somehow that makes you more valuable. But just as with our gifts, wearing less clothing really doesn't make you more special. You might get more attention, but in the end people respect those who are modest. I know it's hard to wait until later in life to see the rewards of your modesty, but it's really worthwhile.**

Say, **Do you remember this verse from last week? Ezekiel 16:14: "And your fame spread among the nations on account of your beauty, because the splendor I had given you made your beauty perfect." Well, there's more to the story. Check this out:**

Reality Check

6. **Ezekiel 16:15: "But you trusted in your beauty and used your fame to become a <u>prostitute</u>."**

Now say, **Ouch! That seems pretty harsh. There's a big long story behind this Scripture, but we'll leave it here. What does a prostitute do? Well, besides the obvious, she dresses a certain way and does her hair and makeup so men will look at her. She uses her outer appearance instead of her inner splendor.**

Then say, **Now clearly, you're significantly different from a prostitute. However, God's point is: When you stop trusting the splendor from your inner beauty to be enough, it's going to cost you. What it seems to be costing most girls these days is their modesty.**

Reality Check

7. 1 Corinthians 6:12 helps bring perspective: "'I have the <u>right</u> to do anything,' you say—but not everything is <u>beneficial</u>."

   Continue, **Check out these crazy verses in Proverbs 5:18-19: "May your fountain be blessed, and may you rejoice in the wife of your youth. A loving doe, a graceful deer—may her breasts satisfy you always, may you ever be intoxicated with her love."**

   Say, **First, note that this refers to a husband and wife. Nothing's wrong with being sexual and nothing's wrong with your body—but being sexual with a male must be in the context of marriage. That said, look what the passage says your body can do to a guy. It can intoxicate him. WOW! What does it mean to be intoxicated?**

   After you get some answers, say, **Intoxication usually refers to being drunk. When someone's drunk, she's not in control of herself. She's not even legally allowed to drive. I say that's some superpower we have—to intoxicate! When we use this power to control men's minds (because of their visual senses) outside of marriage, the results aren't good.**

   Next say, **You have freedom to do what you please. Even when you know what I think, what your parents say, and what God says, you're still free to do what you want.**

Reality Check

8. What you do with your appearance is your choice. But just because you have the <u>freedom</u> to dress and look however you choose, not all ways are <u>beneficial</u>. You teach people how to treat you and perceive you.

9. Ephesians 5:3: "But among you there must not be even a <u>hint</u> of sexual immorality, or of any kind of impurity, or of greed, because these are improper for God's holy people." (NIV)

Say, **When you're on a scavenger hunt, often all you need is a hint to find the item. In the same way, if you have even a hint of sexuality about you, many guys' imaginations will run with that. You aren't telling them they can touch you, but you may be hinting at it without even thinking that way. Some would call this flirting.**

Then say, **God's standards are different than our culture's standards:**

▷ **Romans 14:21: "It is better not to eat meat or drink wine or to do anything else that will cause your brother or sister to fall."**

▷ **1 Corinthians 8:9: "Be careful, however, that the exercise of your rights does not become a stumbling block to the weak."**

Ask, **So does it really matter if guys look at you?**

Explain, **Here's some more of what God says about that. Matthew 5:28: "But I tell you that anyone who looks at a woman lustfully has already committed adultery with her in his heart."**

Reality Check

10. Luke 17:2: "It would be better for you to be thrown into the sea with a millstone tied around your neck than for you to <u>cause</u> one of these little ones to stumble."

Say, **God's not very happy about our going around making life hard on each other. God's not saying everyone who dresses inappropriately should go kill themselves in the ocean. However, God is saying we're doing wrong when we tempt someone else to sin. Matthew 5:28 tells us that when boys are lusting over you, it's sin—so when you dress in a way that draws attention to yourself (not modestly), you're tempting guys.**

Continue, **Check out what Romans 6:12-14 from** *The Message* says:

> That means you must not give sin a vote in the way you conduct your lives. Don't give it the time of day. Don't even run little errands that are connected with that old way of life. Throw yourselves wholeheartedly and full-time—remember, you've been raised from the dead!—into God's way of doing things. Sin can't tell you how to live. After all, you're not living under that old tyranny any longer. You're living in the freedom of God.

Say, **You were created to show God's love. Look at Ephesians 5:3 again: "But among you there must not be even a hint of sexual immorality, or of any kind of impurity, or of greed, because these are improper for God's holy people."**

Ask, **Who are these things improper for? God's holy people. You're holy! Go back to number 9 and circle the word** *holy* **on your outline. Do you know what** *holy* **means?**

After you get some answers, say, **It means "set apart or different." You're God's child. That makes you different from everyone else. It's an honor and should bring you a sense of pride. Consider modesty a badge of honor, a privilege. Because not having to be a slave and needing men's heads to turn your direction to think you're valuable is a privilege.**

Reality Check

11. **A guy who's morally pure and truly seeking to be like God will eventually <u>avoid</u> you because you're <u>poison</u> to his being (if you're using your sex appeal to attract him).**

    Explain, **If you're trying to attract a guy who likes you for your sex appeal, using it to lure him will work very well. But if you're trying to attract a guy who's looking for a girl who's confident in who she is inside and proud of who God made her to be and a guy who wants to be with you for a long time—then that guy will avoid you because you're the opposite of what he's looking for.**

If guys are observing your body more than your splendor, then you may be misusing your body.

TAKE OUT

With the time you have left, talk about ways your girls can use the clothes they already have and wear them more modestly. Maybe bring in magazines or store ads showing pictures of clothes you feel are trendy yet appropriate.

Then give each girl the wrapped up little box with wedding paper to send home with them as reminders that they're more desirable in the long run by the opposite sex if they're fully wrapped. You could even write a little note on each gift that says something like,

> EPHESIANS 5:3: "BUT AMONG YOU THERE MUST NOT BE EVEN A HINT OF SEXUAL IMMORALITY, OR OF ANY KIND OF IMPURITY, OR OF GREED, BECAUSE THESE ARE IMPROPER FOR GOD'S HOLY PEOPLE." or EZEKIEL 16:14 SAYS, "AND YOUR FAME SPREAD AMONG THE NATIONS ON ACCOUNT OF YOUR BEAUTY, BECAUSE THE SPLENDOR I HAD GIVEN YOU MADE YOUR BEAUTY PERFECT DECLARES THE LORD."

Or you could give each girl a little badge to remind her that being modest is a badge of honor.

BECOMING BALANCED: KEEPING YOUR BODY IN CHECK

1. Your superpower is called "sex_____."

2. Each gender has one of the five_____ that's stronger than the other gender's.

    A. Females tend to have a stronger sense of_____.

    B. _____ tends to be a stronger sense for guys.

3. In a given day I see...

    _____ cleavage

    _____ panty edges sticking out of pants

    _____ belly buttons

    _____ bra straps

    _____ skin showing below the belly button

4. To boys you're a walking_____.

5. Modesty is looking normal without drawing_____ to yourself.

6. Ezekiel 16:15: "But you trusted in your beauty and used your fame to become a_____."

7. 1 Corinthians 6:12 helps bring perspective: "'I have the_____ to do anything,' you say—but not everything is_____."

8. What you do with your appearance is your choice. But just because you have the_____ to dress and look however you choose, not all ways are_____. You teach people how to treat you.

9. Ephesians 5:3: "But among you there must not be even a_____ of sexual immorality, or of any kind of impurity, or of greed, because these are improper for God's holy people." (NIV)

10. Luke 17:2: "It would be better for you to be thrown into the sea with a millstone tied around your neck than for you to_____ one of these little ones to stumble."

11. A guy who's morally pure and truly seeking to be like God will eventually_____ you because you're_____ to his being (if you're using your sex appeal to attract him).

BECOMING BALANCED: KEEPING YOUR BODY IN CHECK
Brainteaser

It's your turn for some fun. Here's another chance to be the smart girl. Try this one on your family. Look carefully; it has several steps.

1. Ask the other person to think of a number between 10 and 100 (have your "victim" keep it a secret).

2 Tell your subject to double the number.

3. Have him add 1.

4. Have him multiply by 5.

5. Tell him to add 5.

6. Have him multiply by 10.

7. Now tell your subject to subtract 100 from the number he ended up with and then tell you the result.

   You take off the last two digits and voilà! You're a genius because you'll have the original number.

Soul Work questions

1. How do you feel about your secret power "sex appeal"?

2. Share your thoughts about what you learned on how guys think.

3. If you were to describe what your personal billboard is advertising (honestly), what would your advertisement have said before our lesson?

4. What would you like your "advertisement" to say if it could say something new?

5. How is our appearance like a present?

6. Are you doing anything that hints of sexual immorality and may be giving your billboard a bad ad?

7. Go through your wardrobe and find three outfits you can adapt or change to make them more appropriate. Wear one of these to our class next week and tell us how you made it different. You can look at store ads for ideas—as long as the ideas are modest to start with.

BECOMING OF CHRIST: SELF-WORTH

Masks to place around the room; star and dot stickers; construction paper, markers, and other craft items; *Men in Black* DVD; *You Are Special* (book by Max Lucado)

HELPING PARENTS

This week's lesson requires the help of parents. I've included a letter for you to send out. We're talking about self-worth this week, and parents, hopefully, will take advantage of the opportunity to bond with their daughters. So ahead of time mail out letters to parents asking them to write a letter praising their daughter for who she is and telling her what she does to make them proud. When you finish sending the letters, come back and prepare the lesson.

REVIEW SOUL WORK

Ask them how that crazy brainteaser went.

APPETIZER: TRICKY STICKERS

Give each student one sheet of star stickers and one of dot stickers. Your girls have three minutes to try to place all their stickers on the other players. The tricky thing is that everyone is putting stickers on each other all at the same time. Tell the girls to take the stickers off themselves and put those on others as well. Whoever has the fewest stickers on their clothes and sticker sheets at the end wins. Be sure to tell the girls to leave their stickers on for now.

QUESTIONS AND COMMENTARY

Say, **Today we're talking about self-worth. What's self-worth?**

After receiving some answers, say, **Self-worth has become a buzz-word these days. You might think if you have good or high self-worth then you're arrogant or self-centered. But self-worth is simply understanding your usefulness and value. We often hear people say some person or another has low self-worth or even no self-worth. What does that mean?**

After more answers add, **Say you have a $100 bill. It came straight from the bank and is as crisp as could be. You have a crazy moment and decide to crumple the paper up and bury it in the middle of the sandy beaches off the Atlantic Ocean. How much is that $100 bill worth now? Nothing less. It may cost a lot of time and energy to find that money, but it still has value. No one can take that away.**

Say, **Saying someone has no or low self-worth can be misunderstood. What that actually means is that she's forgotten what she was created for. She hasn't lost any of her value but she has buried it deep within herself—and to find it we just need to go on a treasure hunt.**

Now say, **Let's look at where some people find their value. What makes someone feel important, or why would someone feel important and valuable? Many of these things could be legitimate qualities God gave you—for example, outward appearance, talents, intelligence, etc. Others might be choices you've made about how you'd like to be—for example, sexy, ditzy, prep, jock, gothic, bully, etc.**

Reality Check

1. With a partner list five things people get their worth or their value from.

   A.

   B.

   C.

   D.

   E.

Give them a minute to make their lists and share answers, then say, **We decide who we want to be and try to look and act the part.**

Reality Check

2. We all wear <u>masks</u>.

Ask, **Why do people wear masks at Halloween?** After receiving some answers, ask, **What kind of masks are we talking about here?**

Specialty: Movie Clip

After some answers, show movie clip: *Men in Black.* Any clip where an alien is shown taking off its human skin will work. There's one great clip in which the two main characters are in the morgue checking out one alien that's dying, and the man's face literally lifts off as a mask would. However, the language may or may not be questionable for your church. I've been in churches where either would be the case. As with all movies use your discretion and wisdom. No movie is worth losing your job or getting kicked off the volunteer squad.

After the clip say, **Usually, we try to wear masks or be other people for one reason: We don't like or love who we are, so we're ashamed of the real us and try to hide ourselves.**

Reality Check

3. We wear these masks because we're afraid of <u>rejection</u>.

Say, **The aliens in *Men in Black* had to take on human forms so they weren't turned into science projects or rejected. They just wanted to be accepted. We wear masks because we're afraid of people not liking our real selves if they know what we're really like. If someone knew the real you and didn't like you, that would be very painful.**

Specialty: Mask Making

Get some paper, markers, glitter, and anything else you can gather up and tell your girls they have three minutes and 42 seconds (or the length of one song of your choice) to make masks that resemble what THEY might be wearing to avoid rejection from friends, family, or others. (You may have sixth or seventh graders who really struggle with this abstract idea. Be sure to look around for them and help them out.)

You may have girls tell you they don't wear masks: "What you see is what you get!" They're the ones who are probably wearing the most masks. Don't let them get by with telling you this. Depending on the level of your relationship with the girls, challenge them. Obviously, doing this in a loving and safe way is vital. Nor do you have to share every mask you think they're wearing or even their deepest, darkest, ugliest ones. Try suggesting less serious masks they wear, then let them share their further ideas.

After everyone's done, say, **The problem is we can never be truly happy when we're wearing masks.**

Reality Check

4. **When you wear your masks, no one can <u>reject</u> you, but you don't give anyone the chance to <u>love</u> the real you, either.**

   Say, **However, if someone doesn't like the mask you wear, you feel as if it's no big deal—you're just pretending any-way. Consider this situation: "Hi, my name's Brianna. I'm in seventh grade. My sister Emily is in ninth grade. We get along pretty well most of the time. She gets mad at me for hanging around all the time, and I get mad at her for being bossy. Other than that we really do get along UNLESS Emily has a friend over. I don't understand it, but she, like, totally transforms into this psycho, mean, ugly person I totally hate to be around. She makes rude comments, gives looks that could kill, and I don't even try to join her conversations! I might come out with claw marks. I guess she thinks it's cool not to like her younger sister or something because she's nice unless her friends are with her. I usually try to hang out in my room just to stay away from her. What I don't get is, Emily's a totally cool person, and I'd love to be just like her when she's being herself. If she acts this way when her friends are around (but not me), I can't imagine her making any new friends. But I know people would totally love her if she'd just be herself." What mask would you say Emily is wearing?**

After some responses, say, **Emily was wearing a bully mask. If anyone ever said anything negative to her about how she treated her sister, she could blow it off in her mind because she knows she really doesn't act that way on a normal day. She's also not sure enough of herself to treat her sister with love and respect. She's afraid her friends will think she's...loving or something. But when you put on a mask, you spend a lot of time trying to seem and feel important. Wearing masks is like being on a treadmill. You use up a lot of energy but get nowhere. You burn up all this work and energy just to seem important in the world and by its standards, but at the end of your journey no one knows or loves the real you.**

Then say, **If you're willing to be the real you without your mask, that's awesome because you're able to experience real love. But you'll also be open to people who could very well be lame and not accept you, which is scary. So you need to be let in on the two secrets of finding where real, lasting, significant self-worth comes from.**

Reality Check

5. **The first key to finding your true value, importance, or self-worth is: Do what you were <u>created</u> for!**

   Say, **If you bought a lamp but never plugged it in, what good would it be? How about if your parents bought you a new computer for your schoolwork and set it up in your room, but you insisted on using a typewriter...how stupid would that be? What would you do if I had a watch on but kept asking you what time it was? You'd tell me to look at my watch. Have you ever tried to cut some paper using a bowl? No. That's what scissors are for. Have you ever seen someone use their teeth for something other than eating? Have you ever done it? How about when your toenails need clipped? What do you use? Hopefully, not your teeth! That's why we have clippers.**

   Ask, **So what were you created for?**

After you receive some answers, say, **The Bible tells us many times that we're aliens in this world. What does that mean?**

After you get some answers, say, **We weren't created to live in this world. Obviously, God put us here and created us with a purpose while we're here. But our ultimate purpose is to be with God in heaven. This world is just the "holding tank." So you might wonder: Why did God even make an earth and not just skip it and have us go straight to heaven? If we're aliens on earth and created for heaven, then what about now? What's our purpose here? Why did God create us?**

After you receive some answers, say, **God created us for two reasons.**

Reality Check

6. The main reason God created us is to have a <u>relationship</u> with us.

   Say, **In 1 Corinthians 7:23 Paul tells us we were bought at a high price, and in Romans 8:38-39 he says, "For I am convinced that neither death nor life, neither angels nor demons, neither the present nor the future, nor any powers, neither height nor depth, nor anything else in all creation, will be able to separate us from the love of God that is in Christ Jesus our Lord." You're a prized possession God isn't letting go of!**

   Continue, **Check out Genesis 3:8: "Then the man and his wife heard the sound of the LORD God as he was walking in the garden in the cool of the day, and they hid from the LORD God among the trees of the garden." Adam and Eve could hear God walking near them (of course, in this verse they're hiding from God because they've sinned). This shows that God originally planned on having such a close relationship with us that he wanted to walk in the garden with us. How awesome would that be? Throughout the Bible God talks to people. God desires a real, intimate relationship with us. Most of us don't understand what that really means, and we don't understand God's love for us.**

Now say, **Having a relationship with Christ doesn't mean we have to sit down every day for hours on end praying and memorizing the Bible. These great activities are very beneficial in our lives and certainly help our relationship with Christ. However, our relationship with Jesus is bigger than that. Reading the Bible or praying are actions we do, but they aren't why God loves us. God loves us because God made us. God's name is on us. The most important part of any relationship is loving the other person. Most people have a hard time accepting that God loves them because they don't believe they're lovable. God's love must be real enough to you so it's all you need.**

Continue, **Many people think of God as sitting on one of those spinning office chairs, as a boss at work would. Imagine God this way. Now imagine you've totally screwed up somehow. God turns the chair so God's back is to you. He can't even stand the sight of you. If you pray hard enough and beg for forgiveness enough, God will reluctantly turn the chair back to face you. God has a dirty look on his face to show you how disappointed he is. Then you mess up again. This time it's huge. Guess what God does. There's no way God wants to see your face this time! Maybe if you memorize a whole chapter of the Bible, God'll turn back around...maybe. NO! This isn't how God works. God is love. God's heart leaps for joy when you take a moment to glance his way.**

Reality Check

7. **If God had a wallet, your <u>picture</u> would be right there in it.**

   Say, **Nothing you can do will change God's love for you. 1 John 4:10 tells us we love because God first loved us. Genesis 1:26-27 tells us we were created in God's image. So if we're made in God's image, God is love, and we can love because God loves us, why do you think it's so hard for some people to love themselves?**

   After some discussion say, **With a partner answer questions eight and nine on your outline.**

Reality Check

8. **Check out Ephesians 3:17-19. Paul is praying for people to know God's love: "I pray that you, being rooted and established in love, may have power, together with all the Lord's people, to grasp how wide and long and high and deep is the love of Christ, and to know this love that surpasses knowledge**—*that you may be filled to the measure of all the fullness of God."*

   What fills us? *(Possible answer: knowing God's love)*

9. **When we can grasp this love and accept it, what do you think happens?** *(Possible answers: We feel pretty valuable; no one else's opinion matters; we can be ourselves without fear of rejection.)*

Discuss their answers, then move on to question 10.

10. **The second key to finding your true value, importance, or self-worth is: <u>Becoming</u> like Christ.**

   Say, **Outside of the teenage world, groups of people tend to gravitate to other people like themselves. Neighborhoods are usually grouped by race, ethnicity, economic background, etc. Who you hang around with influences you as well. Have you ever noticed that groups of friends tend to dress the same, act the same, do their hair the same, talk the same, etc.? If you hang around with a group that swears a lot, you're likely to swear, too, even if swear words just slip out.**

   Ask, **Have you ever heard someone say, "That shirt is very becoming on you"? What do you think that means?**

   After some answers say, **It simply means your beauty is revealed through what you're wearing.**

   Go on, **This comes back to the question of what God created us for. We know the first reason is to have a relationship with Jesus. Just as we become like our friends we hang out with, when we have a relationship with Christ and "hang out" with him, we'll become like him. You start becoming like Christ, revealing his beauty. If you become exactly like Jesus (kind, loving, forgiving, never self-seeking, never rude, always including everyone, etc.), then you'll be proud** of who you are. You won't be ashamed of anything about yourself.

Next say, **Whew! It sounds hard because God has so many characteristics. However, as we become more like Christ and less like the world, we'll grow closer and closer to becoming who God created us to be, start to have more self-confidence, and grow in our self-worth by being proud of who we are. As we become more like Jesus, we'll naturally be someone people can't help but want to be around—just as people were with Christ.**

Now say, **God also created us to help others in their relationships with Christ. Acts 20:24 says, "I consider my life worth nothing to me; my only aim is to finish the race and complete the task the Lord Jesus has given me—the task of testifying to the good news of God's grace." 1 Corinthians 10:31 tells us, "So whether you eat or drink or whatever you do, do it all for the glory of God."**

Reality Check

11. **The second reason God created us is to show God's glory. God's glory is simply making the invisible God <u>visible</u> to others.**

   Ask, **What does to "show God's glory" or do things "for the glory of God" mean?**

   After you get some answers, say, **We were all born with the same capability to love others and bring significant improvements to this world—make it a better place. You have the power to bring joy into other people's lives. Doing things for the "glory of God" or showing "God's glory" is when we live in a way so people see who God is and see God's love in us. Then the invisible God becomes visible. This is our job—to love God and show others God's love, too.**

Say, **Philippians 4:11-13 says—**

> I have learned to be content whatever the circumstances. I know what it is to be in need, and I know what it is to have plenty. I have learned the secret of being content in any and every situation, whether well fed or hungry,

whether living in plenty or in want. I can do all this through him who gives me strength.

Add, **This won't come easily or naturally because our culture trains us to want more stuff. Living God's way is a choice you have to make. But once we understand how much God loves us, then we can show God's love to others. That's key to our feeling valuable—making God's love, something invisible, visible to others. How do we do this?**

After you receive some answers, say, **This also could be as easy as accepting people who others don't accept or being slow to anger with our parents—or as hard as serving others in millions of various ways, such as inviting an outcast to your birthday party...then giving all your presents to an orphanage.**

Say, **You might be wondering, "But how can I make that choice every day when it's so hard to remember and not get caught up in this world?" I'm so glad you asked! Psalm 46:10 tells us the secret to believing God's love for us: "Be still and know that I am God." Listen for God. Rest assured knowing you're valuable, and God has a reason and a plan for your life.**

Now say, **Philippians 3:12-14 helps us, too: "Not that I have already obtained all this, or have already arrived at my goal...Forgetting what is behind and straining toward what is ahead, I press on toward the goal." This isn't easy. We're not like Christ yet. Thankfully, we don't have to wait until we are like him to have good self-worth. Keep working and making wise choices. You can be proud of who you are as you press on and see a good work being done in you, as you see Christ's beauty instead of your own.**

Specialty: Max Lucado Reading (Option)

If you have a longer small group time, you can have the luxury of reading *You Are Special* by Max Lucado. The rest of us will need to show the book and summarize the story: **God wants to help you stop caring about what others think; instead God wants you to find the joy and freedom that comes from living only to please God. As you let Jesus be** the only person who matters to you, all those masks and others' opinions will come off, and you'll become proud of who God made you to be. This is when you'll be radiant with love. You will be truly becoming of Christ.

Reality Check

12. You are perfect as you are because you were created to <u>become</u> of Christ.

TAKE OUT

Instruct your girls to take their masks home and put them on or by their doors, but first have them take some of the dots and stars still stuck on themselves and put those on their masks as well. Say, **Look around. If each star and dot represents our worth and value, how would we be doing? In real life we do just that with people, only using our words and actions instead of stickers. Use your mask as a reminder that you don't need to pretend to be someone you aren't. Even when people judge you in ways that make you feel good or bad, your value can't be based on those things. When you walk out your door, remind yourself that the mask is staying in your room—you're not taking it with you.**

DEAR [PARENT NAMES]

I've been enjoying your daughter in my small group this semester. I really feel we're addressing issues at the heart of being a middle school girl. My purpose in this letter is to give you an opportunity to be involved with this week's lesson and encourage your daughter.

This week we're talking about self-worth. We'll be looking at our true selves, good and bad, and finding our worth in the fact that God made us and loves us incredibly. When we focus on God, we start to focus less on others' opinions of us and become more confident in who we are. One of the things the girls will be doing for their Soul Work (it's our class homework but called that to sound less school-ish) is to write letters telling how they see their true selves. They'll include strengths, weaknesses, and character issues.

The major goal of the letter is to figure out who the real person is under all the "masks." We've talked about how each of them is who God created her to be and how she has value because she's a masterpiece of God. But we have to know who she is before we can be proud of her. Often when the girls sit down to write their letters, they struggle to find many things they actually like about themselves. This is where I need your help!

I'm asking you to write your daughter a letter, too, though she won't know about this until she receives it. You can choose to write this as a couple or each write a letter individually. No one knows your daughter better than you. You can see her outward beauty as well as her inward beauty. You see her strengths in the midst of her weaknesses. You see her potential. You see how God has created your daughter to be unique, and you wouldn't trade her for anyone else in the world. Please take this opportunity to praise her, encourage her, and instill value in who she is.

Your daughter has a place in her Soul Work where she's encouraged to ask your opinion on how you view her. I encourage you to read her your letter at that time. You may want to ask to read her letter if she's willing (though don't require her) to share it. This could be a very intimate time for you. I guarantee your daughter will keep your letter for years and years, so please don't use this letter to try and help her see where she needs to improve. She'd reread those comments and hear you telling her she's not good enough. If your daughter never asks you what you think because she feels awkward or hasn't had time to get her Soul Work done, put your letter in an envelope and tell her it's a note to give me in class. Then I'll give it to her at an appropriate time during class.

Thank you for your support and for making this a priority for your daughter. If I can do anything for you or your daughter, please let me know.

Working by your side,

BECOMING OF CHRIST: SELF-WORTH

1. With a partner list five things people get their worth or their value from.

   A. _____

   B. _____

   C. _____

   D. _____

   E. _____

2. We all wear_____.

3. We wear these masks because we're afraid of_____.

4. When you wear your masks, no one can_____ you, but you don't give anyone the chance to_____ the real you, either.

5. The first key to finding your true value, importance, or self-worth is: Do what you were_____ for!

6. The main reason God created us is to have a_____ with us.

7. If God had a wallet, your_____ would be right there in it.

8. Check out Ephesians 3:17-19. Paul is praying for people to know God's love.

   "I pray that you, being rooted and established in love, may have power, together with all the Lord's people to grasp how wide and long and high and deep is the love of Christ, and to know this love that surpasses knowledge—that you may be filled to the measure of all the fullness of God."

   What fills us?

9. When we can grasp this love and accept it, what do you think happens?

10. The second key to finding your true value, importance, or self-worth is: _____ like Christ.

11. The second reason God created us is to show God's glory. God's glory is simply making the invisible God_____ to others.

12. You are perfect as you are because you were created to_____ of Christ.

BECOMING OF CHRIST: SELF-WORTH

Get your favorite snack, most comfortable slippers, and the coolest pen in your house and let's get started.

Brainteaser

A man went into a hardware store and was looking for an item when the clerk walked up and asked, "Yes, sir, may I help you?" "Yes," said the man. How much are these?" "They're 25 cents each, so you can get 25 for 50 cents and 114 for 75 cents."

What were the items?

This is a hard one so you may want to get some help from your friends and parents.

Soul Work questions

1. During class we talked about how we all wear masks. Why do we do this (besides dressing up for Halloween)?

2. What do you pretend to be but really aren't?

3. Why can't we ever be happy when we wear our masks?

4. What are the two keys to having a healthy self-worth? Hint: See numbers 5 and 10 on your Reality Check sheet.

5. This week write a letter to yourself and/or God describing yourself. This letter should include things you think you're good at and things you love about yourself. Include things you do that are good for others and any accomplishments you're proud of. Also talk about any weaknesses you think you have. Describe the real you, without masks— not the person you wish you were but the real person deep down inside you who possibly no one knows. If you're going to risk being loved and love yourself for who you are, then you need to know who you really are. This letter will not be shared with anyone unless you want to share it with the group, your parents, or anyone you choose. So try to be very honest. Remember: God loves you for exactly who you are, good and bad (not to mention he already knows you as you are).

6. When your letter is finished, NOT before you've written it, go to your parents and ask them who they think God created you to be, who they see as the real you. No one knows you better than your own parents, believe it or not. No one cherishes you more than they do. Their opinions are very valuable and probably right on target. Really, I want you to go do this!

CHAPTER EIGHT

BECOMING IN TUNE: FEELINGS

INGREDIENTS

Items for game (noodles, dry beans, yarn, jewelry, dirt, chocolate chips, M&M's, etc.); several little bags, boxes, or bowls, one for each game item; *City of Angels* DVD; one snack-sized baggie of fake grass (as used in Easter baskets) per girl in your group

REVIEW SOUL WORK

Here's the answer for your brainteaser: house numbers (that's what the store was selling, each number for a quarter). If you had any parents give you letters to deliver be sure to do that after the study is over (and privately). Also note those students whose parents didn't write letters to them—and then write those students this week in place of the parent letters.

APPETIZER: WHAT'S IN THE BOX?

Bring several bowls or boxes, each containing an item for the girls to guess what it is. Cover each container with a towel so there's no peeking. The girls may use only one hand to feel the items. Have the girls write down their answers. Some examples of these items: noodles, dry beans, yarn, jewelry, dirt, chocolate chips, M&M's. But anything small that fits in your bowls or boxes will work.

After the game say, **Today we're talking about feelings. However, we won't be talking about feeling with our hands—but feelings in the sense of emotions. Has anyone ever told you you seem as if you're in a bad mood? Do you notice when someone is down? Maybe you're the one who tells other people when they're in bad moods. Girls are often more aware of others' feelings than their own. God made most girls a little more compassionate and tender than most boys. God's given you all an incredible gift by giving you feelings. However, feelings can sometimes be hard to live with.**

QUESTIONS AND COMMENTARY

Ask, **What are feelings? We hear about them all the time: "I'm feeling sick." "I have a feeling it's going to rain." "I had my feelings hurt." "I'm feeling sad." "I'm feeling happy." Let's list as many feelings as we can think of.**

If you have a chalkboard or whiteboard, have the girls go write whatever feelings they can think of on it. Otherwise you can use a poster board. Or if you don't have anything to write on or don't want to, have the girls yell the feelings out. *(Possible answers: happy, sad, tired, loneliness, angry, jealous, love, hate, homesick, thirsty, hungry, pain, comfort, eager, ambitious, curious, compassion, thankfulness, frustration, etc.)*

Ask, **Which feelings we listed are good?** Circle these with one color.

Which ones are bad? Circle these with a different color.

Then say, **They're actually all good. Feelings are gifts from God to help you. We'll refer to them as positive and negative (rather than good and bad) because some warn us of positive things and others warn us of negative things. Can you think of ways feelings help us?**

Specialty: Movie Clip

After you get some answers, set up the movie clip: **This is a movie about an angel who gives up his chance to live forever so he can have feelings. At the end the angel is asked "Was it worth it?"** Show the movie clip: *City of Angels* (1:35 Seth on the couch to 1:39 "than an eternity without it").

After the clip say, **The Bible has a lot of examples of how feelings help us. Here's one. Remember the Good Samaritan? Luke 10:25-37 tells us the story. Can anyone summarize it for me?**

After you hear a summary, **say, Verse 33 tells us that while the Samaritan is traveling, he sees the beat-up man and has compassion on him. These men's countries hated each other, yet one was able to have compassion and show the other love. Remember our big jobs in life? To love God and love others to show them the invisible God. This Samaritan's feelings made this possible.**

Continue, **Often our emotions or feelings seem to get us in trouble. What's an example of a feeling gone bad or a negative feeling?**

After you hear some examples, say, **Every example you can think of is actually the action, or the result, of the feeling that made a mess of things.**

Reality Check

1. **Feelings and emotions are our <u>radar</u> system. They warn us about what's going on inside us and in our lives.**

   Say, **Radar can predict the weather. Because of some crazy machines, some person on TV can tell me how warm or cold it's going to be or whether it's going to snow, rain, or be sunny, or if a tornado will hit me in 10 minutes. All this is done with radar. Radar can't change the weather or stop a tornado, but it can tell us what's going on and warn us about what's ahead so we can be prepared. The meteorologist doesn't determine the weather. She analyzes the radar signals and reports what's coming.**

   Now say, **Think about pain. Wouldn't it be nice if we never felt pain?**

   After you get some answers, say, **Would it? When someone feels sick, he can go to a doctor. Doctors are able to find illnesses, cancer, or tumors and heal many problems because people feel sick—and that's how they know something's wrong. When you break a bone, it hurts! You go and get it fixed. If you didn't feel as if anything hurts or is wrong and then didn't go to the doctor, you wouldn't function properly because your ailment wouldn't heal properly.**

   Explain, **Feelings work the same way. They're warning signs for us. They tell us when something's good or wrong.**

Reality Check

2. **Emotions make terrible masters but are great <u>servants</u>.**

Ask, **What does that mean? How would this be true? In other words, can the meteorologist ever make a tornado using the radar system? Can she make it rain?**

When you get some answers, say, **No, she can only tell us what's already going on. The radar system isn't in control. But it makes a great tool when used properly. So let's learn how to use your feelings and emotions properly.**

Then say, **We know they're good but they seem to get us into so much trouble. Here's the key to how we can use feelings and emotions and stay in control of them.**

Reality Check

3. Ask, **"What are my feelings trying to <u>tell</u> me?"**

   Say, **When someone has abused a child, we get angry and even feel rage. These emotions are from God—he created you with emotions. They help us know when something's wrong. So when we get angry about abuse, we know it's wrong and can do something to help the child, such as reporting the abuse. Jesus saw people misusing the temple, and he got angry because it was wrong.** Have someone read Mark 11:15-18 (Jesus clearing the temple). After the passage is read, ask, **Was clearing the temple okay for Jesus to do?**

   After some discussion say, **Jesus was angry about how people were using the temple. Now if Jesus had started chopping off people's heads for misusing the temple, that would've been wrong. If a person went out and murdered a person who molested a child, that's wrong. These are both actions. The feeling of anger was the same when Jesus cleared the temple and when someone reported an abuser, but what they did with the feeling was different from chopping off heads and committing murder.**

   Say, **Jesus' anger warned him that the misuse of the temple was wrong, which led him to clear out the temple to try to restore order. This was good. When we're angry about a child being abused, it's a good warning sign from our feelings about the situation being bad and the child needing help. However, killing the person who abused the child would be** a bad action. Finding help for the child and prosecuting the abuser would be good outcomes or actions.

Ask, **How did feelings help these two situations have good outcomes? What would've happened if the people in these situations had no feelings? Or what would've happened if the people had only feelings and no logic?**

After some discussion say, **Feelings are good. When people become numb to their feelings, that's when they often fall into addictions. Take alcohol, for example. It produces false feelings. You suddenly feel brave or happy, but you're not actually brave or happy. So when the alcohol wears off, you stop feeling brave or happy or look for more alcohol so you can feel brave or happy again. You become dependent on these false feelings. Often people who lose their ability to have real feelings also become suicidal.**

Continue, **On the good side, feelings are why we can love friends, family, pets, and God. We need feelings to function in life. But our enjoyable feelings in life are usually easier to deal with than our negative ones. When we're happy, in love, thankful, etc., our actions are usually good.**

Reality Check

A. **What's a positive feeling you have? Write down a situation you feel good about: someone you love, something you're thankful for, something that's going well in your life, etc.**

After a minute or so say, **Often our feelings are trying to warn us about negative things. They're trying to help us be safe and happy. However, even positive emotions can be telling us something. If our parents let us go spend the night at our friend's house, we can take the happiness and excitement as reminders to thank Mom and Dad or even do something special for them in return. If we're in love, we can use that good feeling and tell God thanks for the joy of love.**

Say, **Our feelings are our radars in life. For example, when you get on a roller coaster, you may feel the fear of danger to your body. Even if it sounds like fun, your feelings may tell you fun isn't good right now. You hear, "DANGER, DANGER!" Those feelings inform you about what's going on in life and help you prepare for what's coming—good or bad.**

Reality Check

B. Now tell a partner a situation in your life you spend a lot of time worrying about or feel strongly about—feelings of anger, worry, fear, stress, pain, jealousy, etc.

C. Are these feelings trying to tell you something?

After the girls have had some time to answer B and C, say, **Feelings are wonderful but become hard to live with when they're not properly channeled. When we ignore our radar and we don't question or analyze our feelings, they can start to get out of hand. They can take over our ability to think clearly.**

Reality Check

4. Do the "green grass" test—a reality check.

Say, **What color is grass? Unless it's dead, it's green. If I told you grass is blue, what would you say? What if I said purple? Pink? What if I had a good argument and was very convincing—would this mean grass is any color other than green? What if I'd convinced many people this was true and maybe even you thought I must be right—would grass no longer be green? Of course not! The truth is, grass is green. Our feelings, our radar system, tell us what's going on in our lives; however, feelings need to be put through a reality test or a "green grass" test. For example, my best friend might yell at me, and I may feel as if my best friend has really gone too far this time. I can let my emotions or feelings get out of control. I can choose to treat her horribly. If so, I've become a slave to my feelings. I let them control my actions and stop me from thinking clearly. The reality check or the "green grass" test would tell me my friend isn't trying to ruin my day. She's simply having a bad day. Her mom totally chewed her out for no reason before school today. Doing this reality check slows my explosion and helps me no longer be a slave to my emotions—rather, I'm free from their control. This is the logic part of the equation we were talking about earlier.**

John 8:32 says, "You will know the truth and the truth will set you free." (Have the girls circle the word *truth* on their **Reality Check** sheets.)

Reality Check

A. We should always ask ourselves, "Is what I'm feeling making sense with real life? Is this emotion equal to the circumstance that caused it?"

Give a personal example of a time when you may have acted a little out of control for the reality of the situation!

Reality Check

B. Ask yourself how much you're in <u>control</u> of your emotions.

1. I'm in <u>total</u> control.

2. I'm a <u>little</u> out of control.

3. I'm totally <u>out</u> of control.

Now instruct the girls: **Consider the situation you told your partner a minute ago (for 3B) that's causing you some hard feelings to deal with. Write down the number one, two, or three according to how in control of that emotion you are beside the letter "C" on your Reality Check sheets.**

Leader Note: *Middle school girls have a lot going on. The girls find it hard to be in control of their feelings and emotions. They feel each emotion very intensely, as if each situation could be the end of the world. Girls especially struggle with being mean. They tend to take out their frustrations on everyone else. All the hormonal stuff going on in their bodies causes a lot of this. However, this is why you need to step in and encourage them to sit back and learn to ask, "In my situation, does it make sense to be mean to everyone around me who has nothing to do with the situation? Why am I being mean to everyone just because I'm mad at so-and-so? Why do I have a bad attitude all the time just because...? Why is my whole day ruined just because...?" Help them understand they have the ability to control their emotions.*

Continue, **You're ready to take one more step. When a meteorologist looks at the radar and tells us a tornado's coming, what do we do? We take appropriate action—getting to the basement, for example. We've looked at the actions you may have taken in** the past, but once you learn to review whether what you're doing is appropriate and figure out whether you're in control, the last step is deciding...

Reality Check

5. **What's the appropriate <u>action</u> for the feelings I'm having?**

   After some answers, say, **On a scale of one to 10—where one means bad: "I take out my negative feelings on others all the time," and 10 means you have a lot of control and usually think about your emotions before you act—raise your hands in the air, indicating how well you think you're doing at using your negative emotions for good. Count from one to 10 and have the girls raise their hands according to what number you're saying. (You can let the girls close their eyes during this exercise so no one sees each other's answers if that'll make it easier for them to be honest.)**

Reality Check

6. **Galatians 5:22-23: "The <u>fruit</u> of the Spirit is love, joy, peace, patience, kindness, goodness, faithfulness, gentleness and self-control."**

   What are these fruits all about? Explain, **How do you tell if an apple tree is a good apple tree? It makes good apples. What kind of tree would it be if it made no apples? Not really an apple tree. If you're doing your job (loving God and making God visible to others), you'll start to see these fruits—of the Spirit—in yourself.**

   Say, **If you're not seeing these qualities in yourself, then you may want to take a second to reevaluate how you're handling your emotions and feelings. Try to get a grip on them and formulate a plan on what more positive responses or actions would be.** Have your girls answer question 7 on their **Reality Check** outlines on their own.

Reality Check

7. **Evaluate your feelings by...**

    A. **Asking, what are my feelings warning me of?**

    B. **Doing the "green grass" test—a reality check.**

    1. **Is what I'm feeling making sense with real life? Is this emotion equal to the circumstance that caused it?**

    2. **Which of these is true?**

        a. **I'm in total control.**

        b. **I'm a little out of control.**

        c. **I'm totally out of control.**

    C. **Thinking about how this feeling and situation can be used to love God and/or make the invisible God visible.**

    D. **Asking, what fruits of the Spirit am I displaying as a result of the actions my feelings produced? If you can't see any fruit of the Spirit, review A and B.**

Before you wrap things up, let your girls know if this is the end of the line for the series (if you're stopping with this book), or if you're continuing the conversation with the sequel, *Living as a Young Woman of God*.

Either way, thank your girls for their hard work and commitment and make sure to pray for each girl individually (and out loud) before you conclude the meeting.

TAKE OUT

Pass out to each girl a snack-sized baggie of that fake grass you get at Easter in your Easter basket (that no one likes because it just takes up too much room and makes less room for candy and stuff) or some other fake grass from a craft department. Tell the girls, **You need to keep this somewhere nearby for when you find yourself out of control of your emotions—in your backpack, locker, or bedroom—or maybe it would be best to just tape it to your forehead! Use it as a reminder of the "green grass" test and remember to evaluate your feelings.**

REALITY CHECK

BECOMING IN TUNE: FEELINGS

1. Feelings and emotions are our_____ system. They warn us about what's going on inside us and in our lives.

2. Emotions make terrible masters but are great_____.

3. Ask, "What are my feelings trying to_____ me?"

   A. What's a positive feeling you have? Write down a situation you feel good about: someone you love, something you're thankful for, something that's going well in your life, etc.

   B. Now tell a partner a situation in your life you spend a lot of time worrying about or feel strongly about—feelings of anger, worry, fear, stress, pain, jealousy, etc.

   C. Are these feelings trying to tell you something?

4. Do the "_____" test—a reality check.

   John 8:32 says, "You will know the truth and the truth will set you free."

   A. We should always ask ourselves, "Is what I'm feeling making sense with real life? Is this emotion equal to the circumstance that caused it?"

   B. Ask yourself how much you're in_____ of your emotions.

      1. I'm in_____ control.

      2. I'm a_____ out of control.

      3. I'm totally_____ of control.

   C._____

5. What's the appropriate_____ for the feelings I'm having?

6. Galatians 5:22-23: "The_____ of the Spirit is love, joy, peace, patience, kindness, goodness, faithfulness, gentleness and self-control."

Get it all in review.

7. Evaluate your feelings by...

A. Asking, what are my feelings warning me of?

B. Doing the "green grass" test—a reality check.

1. Is what I'm feeling making sense with real life? Is this emotion equal to the circumstance that caused it?

2. Which of these is true?

a. I'm in total control.

b. I'm a little out of control.

c. I'm totally out of control.

C. Thinking about how this feeling and situation can be used to love God and/or make the invisible God visible.

D. Asking, what fruits of the Spirit am I displaying as a result of the actions my feelings produced? If you can't see any fruit of the Spirit, review A and B.

SOUL WORK

BECOMING IN TUNE: FEELINGS

Brainteaser

Time to get you thinking!

There was a wreck. A man in a small foreign car was at fault because he'd darted out in front of a big car, causing it to crash through a store window. The people in the foreign car were unhurt. In the other car one person was injured and one died. A manslaughter charge was never filed against the driver of the foreign car. Why?

Soul Work questions

Your **Soul Work** for this week is a little different than usual. I want you to journal each day. Some days you'll be quick and others you'll need to take longer. I want you to use some of the questions we used in class. So feel free to refer back to your Reality Check sheets if you need to see how this works.

Here's the basic outline for each day.

1. Write down a feeling (positive or negative) you had today. Writing out the whole situation that caused the feeling is often helpful. Then try to answer the rest of the questions honestly about this feeling and situation; be sure to write down all your answers.

2. What are my feelings warning me of?

3. Do the "green grass" test.

   A. Is what I'm feeling making sense with real life? Is this emotion equal to the circum-stance that caused it?

   B. Which of these is true?

      1. I'm in total control.

      2. I'm a little out of control.

      3. I'm totally out of control.

4. Think about how this feeling and situation can be used to love God and/or make the invisible God visible.

5. What fruits of the Spirit am I displaying as a result of the actions my feelings pro-duced? If you can't see any fruit of the Spirit, review 3A and B.

6. Choose one of the situations you journal about this week and ask one or both of your parents for advice about it. You don't need to ask for advice on how to fix the problem; just tell them you're evaluating what you're feeling and want to know if they think you should be aware of anything more those feelings might be trying to tell you. Write down their thoughts.

Remember to do this process (questions one through five) once every day.